2nd EDITION

Ventures

WORKBOOK

BASIC

Gretchen Bitterlin   Dennis Johnson   Donna Price   Sylvia Ramirez

K. Lynn Savage (Series Editor)

with Kathleen Olson

CAMBRIDGE
UNIVERSITY PRESS

CAMBRIDGE UNIVERSITY PRESS
Cambridge, New York, Melbourne, Madrid, Cape Town,
Singapore, São Paulo, Delhi, Mexico City

Cambridge University Press
32 Avenue of the Americas, New York, NY 10013-2473, USA

www.cambridge.org
Information on this title: www.cambridge.org/9781107691087

First published 2008

Printed in Mexico by Quad / Graphics Querétaro, S.A. de C.V.

A catalog record for this publication is available from the British Library.

ISBN 978-1-107-64102-0 Student's Book with Audio CD
ISBN 978-1-107-69108-7 Workbook with Audio CD
ISBN 978-1-139-88532-4 Online Workbook
ISBN 978-1-107-67608-4 Teacher's Edition with Audio CD / CD-ROM
ISBN 978-1-107-66806-5 Class Audio CDs
ISBN 978-1-107-61622-6 Presentation Plus

Additional resources for this publication at www.cambridge.org/ventures

Art direction, book design, photo research, and layout services: Q2A / Bill Smith
Audio production: CityVox, LLC

Contents

Welcome

1 Write the letters.

A B C *D* E F

G ___ I J K ___

M N O ___ Q R

S ___ U V W ___

Y Z

2 Write the letters.

a b *c* d e ___

g h ___ j k ___

m n ___ p q ___

s t ___ v w ___

y z

Check your answers. See page 131.

3 Listen and number.

TRACK 2

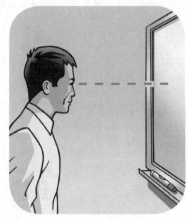

a. _1_

b. ____

c. ____

d. ____

e. ____

f. ____

g. ____

h. ____

i. ____

Check your answers. See page 131.

4 Write the numbers.

_1_	**2**	**3**	___	**5**
6	___	**8**	**9**	___
11	**12**	___	**14**	**15**
___	**17**	**18**	___	**20**

5 Write the numbers.

one	two	___
four	___	six
___	eight	___
ten	eleven	___
thirteen	___	fifteen
___	seventeen	___
nineteen	___	

Check your answers. See page 131.

6 **Look at the pictures. Write the numbers.**

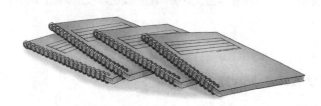

1. ___*four*___

2. _____

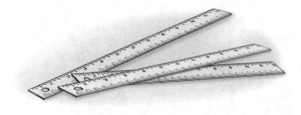

3. _____

4. _____

5. _____

6. _____

7. _____

8. _____

Check your answers. See page 131.

LESSON A Listening

1 Look at the ID card. Write the words.

Student ID Card

1 *Anna*
first name

2 *Lopez*
last name

3 *Mexico*
country

4 *254*
area code

5 *555-2992*
phone number

1. _f_ _i_ _r_ _s_ _t_   _n_ _a_ _m_ _e_

2. ___ ___ ___ ___   ___ ___ ___ ___

3. ___ ___ ___ ___ ___ ___ ___

4. ___ ___ ___ ___   ___ ___ ___ ___

5. ___ ___ ___ ___ ___ ___   ___ ___ ___ ___ ___ ___

2 Write the words from Exercise 1.

1. _A_ _n_ _n_ _a_
first name

2. ___ ___ ___ ___ ___
last name

3. ___ ___ ___ ___ ___ ___
country

4. ___ ___ ___
area code

5. ___ ___ ___ - ___ ___ ___ ___
phone number

Check your answers. See page 131.

3 **Listen and write the number.**

TRACK 3

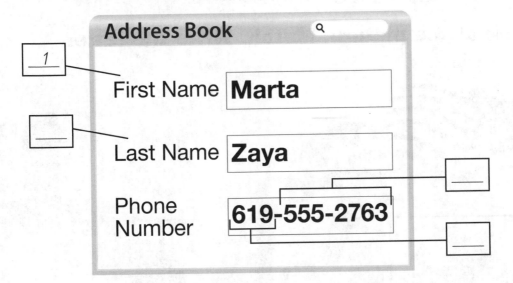

Address Book

First Name **Marta**

Last Name **Zaya**

Phone Number **619-555-2763**

_1_

---

4 **Write the words.**

| area code | first name | last name | phone number |

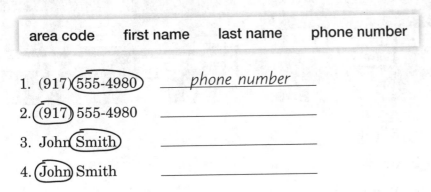

1. (917) 555-4980   _phone number_

2. (917) 555-4980   _____

3. John Smith   _____

4. John Smith   _____

---

5 **Write the words.**

| area code | first name | last name | phone number |

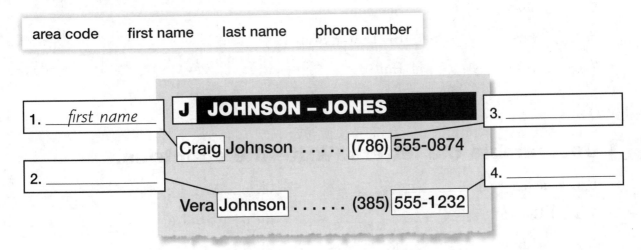

1. _first name_

J JOHNSON – JONES

Craig Johnson . . . . . (786) 555-0874

3. _____

2. _____

Vera Johnson . . . . . . (385) 555-1232

4. _____

Check your answers. See page 131.

LESSON B Countries

1 Look at the picture. Match. Write the letter.

1. _f_ Diane   a. Brazil

2. ____ Fabio   b. China

3. ____ Kalifa   c. Mexico

4. ____ Lorena   d. Russia

5. ____ Shen   e. Somalia

6. ____ Yuri   f. the United States

7. ____ Binh   g. Haiti

8. ____ Flore   h. Vietnam

2 Unscramble the letters. Write the countries.

1. C n a h i   _____

2. z i l B a r   _____

3. s s i a R u   _____

4. e x M i o c   _____

5. o m S l i a a   _____

6. i H i t a   _____

Check your answers. See page 131.

3 **Look at the picture. Write the countries.**

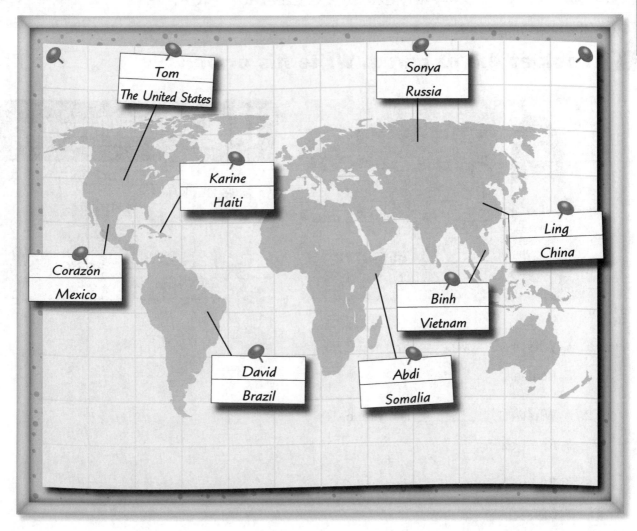

1. Where is Abdi from?   _____*Somalia*_____.

2. Where is Tom from?   _____.

3. Where is Ling from?   _____.

4. Where is David from?   _____.

5. Where is Sonya from?   _____.

6. Where is Corazón from? _____.

7. Where is Karine from?   _____.

8. Where is Binh from?   _____.

Check your answers. See page 131.

Study the chart on page 126.

1 **Look at the ID cards. Write *his* or *her*.**

1. *A* What's _____*her*_____ first name?

   B Louise.

2. *A* What's _____ last name?

   B Ramirez.

3. *A* What's _____ area code?

   B 614.

4. *A* What's _____ phone number?

   B 555-9770.

5. *A* What's _____ area code?

   B 825.

6. *A* What's _____ first name?

   B Carlos.

7. *A* What's _____ last name?

   B Miller.

8. *A* What's _____ phone number?

   B 555-8052.

Check your answers. See page 131.

2 Write *My* or *your*.

Alan What's _____your_____ first name?
1

Manuel _____ first name is Manuel.
2

Alan What's _____ last name?
3

Manuel _____ last name is Alvez.
4

Alan What's _____ area code?
5

Manuel _____ area code is 917.
6

Alan What's _____ phone number?
7

Manuel _____ phone number is 555-9845.
8

3 Complete the form about Manuel.

Job Interview Notes

First name: _____ *Manuel* _____

Last name: _____

Area code: _____

Phone number: _____

Check your answers. See page 131.

LESSON **D** Reading

1 Circle the answers.

Hello

First name	*Boris*
Last name	*Egorov*
Country	*Russia*

1. His name is _____ .   (Boris Egorov)   Egorov Boris

2. His last name is _____ .   Boris   Egorov

3. His first name is _____ .   Boris   Egorov

4. He is from _____ .   Russia   country

2 Match. Write the letter.

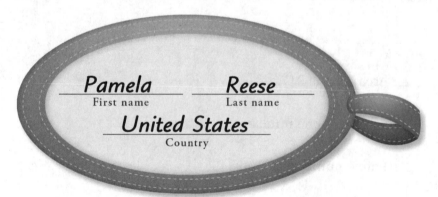

Pamela   *Reese*
First name   Last name

United States
Country

1. __c__ What's her name?   a. Reese

2. ____ What's her last name?   b. the United States

3. ____ What's her first name?   c. Pamela Reese

4. ____ Where is she from?   d. Pamela

Check your answers. See page 131.

3 **Complete the calendar.**

JANUARY
1	2	3	4	5
6	7	8	9	10	11	12
13	14	15	16	17	18	19
20	21	22	23	24	25	26
27	28	29	30	31

February
1	2
3	4	5	6	7	8	9
10	11	12	13	14	15	16
17	18	19	20	21	22	23
24	25	26	27	28	29

(March)
| 1 |
2	3	4	5	6	7	8
9	10	11	12	13	14	15
16	17	18	19	20	21	22
23	24	25	26	27	28	29
30	31

APRIL
1	2	3	4	5
6	7	8	9	10	11	12
13	14	15	16	17	18	19
20	21	22	23	24	25	26
27	28	29	30

(May)
1	2	3
4	5	6	7	8	9	10
11	12	13	14	15	16	17
18	19	20	21	22	23	24
25	26	27	28	29	30	31

(June)
1	2	3	4	5	6	7
8	9	10	11	12	13	14
15	16	17	18	19	20	21
22	23	24	25	26	27	28
29	30

JULY
1	2	3	4	5
6	7	8	9	10	11	12
13	14	15	16	17	18	19
20	21	22	23	24	25	26
27	28	29	30	31

(August)
1	2
3	4	5	6	7	8	9
10	11	12	13	14	15	16
17	18	19	20	21	22	23
24	25	26	27	28	29	30
31

(September)
1	2	3	4	5	6
7	8	9	10	11	12	13
14	15	16	17	18	19	20
21	22	23	24	25	26	27
28	29	30	31

OCTOBER
1	2	3	4
5	6	7	8	9	10	11
12	13	14	15	16	17	18
19	20	21	22	23	24	25
26	27	28	29	30	31

(November)
| 1 |
2	3	4	5	6	7	8
9	10	11	12	13	14	15
16	17	18	19	20	21	22
23	24	25	26	27	28	29
30	31

DECEMBER
1	2	3	4	5	6
7	8	9	10	11	12	13
14	15	16	17	18	19	20
21	22	23	24	25	26	27
28	29	30	31

4 **Read. Write the answers. Then listen.**

TRACK 4

Birthdays in Group 1

January: Lynn   April: Tony
February: Diego   June: Jim
July: Tina

1. When is Jim's birthday? *In June* .
2. When is Lynn's birthday? _____ .
3. When is Diego's birthday? _____ .
4. When is Tony's birthday? _____ .
5. When is Tina's birthday? _____ .

UNIT 1   **13**

LESSON E Writing

1 Complete the words.

area code	country	first name	last name	phone number

1. c <u>o</u> <u>u</u> <u>n</u> <u>t</u> <u>r</u> <u>y</u>

2. a ___ ___ ___   c ___ ___ ___

3. f ___ ___ ___ ___   n ___ ___ ___

4. p ___ ___ ___ ___   n ___ ___ ___ ___ ___

5. l ___ ___   n ___ ___ ___

2 Look at the ID card. Complete the sentences.

1. Her _____<u>first</u>_____ _____<u>name</u>_____ is Mei.

2. Her _____ _____ is Wu.

3. Her _____ _____ is 773.

4. Her _____ _____ is 555-1173.

5. She is from _____.

Check your answers. See page 132.

3 Look at the ID card. Complete the sentences.

Springfield Library

Emma
First name

Harris
Last name

(407)
Area code

555-6524
Phone number

1. Her first name is _____ *Emma* _____.

2. Her last name is _____.

3. Her area code is _____.

4. Her phone number is _____.

4 Read. Complete the driver's license. Then listen.

TRACK 5

Meet the new student at River Valley Driving School. His first name is Octavio. His last name is Diaz. He is from Mexico. His area code is 206. His phone number is 555-3687. His birthday is December 7, 1995.

INTERNATIONAL DRIVER'S LICENSE

Octavio
First name

_____
Last name

_____
Date of birth (birthday)

_____
Place of birth (country)

_____
Area code

_____
Phone number

LESSON F Another view

```
              Adult English Program
                 Registration Form
                  September 2013

   Name:    Camila Silva

   Address:  2000 Chicago Avenue

            Oak Park, IL  60304

   Phone:   (708) 555-1979

   Birthday:  October 16, 1992

   Country:  Brazil

   Signature:  Camila Silva
```

1. Her last name is _____.
   Ⓐ Park
   Ⓑ Camila
   ● Silva

2. Her area code is _____.
   Ⓐ 60304
   Ⓑ 708
   Ⓒ 555

3. She is from _____.
   Ⓐ Brazil
   Ⓑ Chicago Avenue
   Ⓒ October

4. Her first name is _____.
   Ⓐ Camila
   Ⓑ Silva
   Ⓒ Oak

5. Her phone number is _____.
   Ⓐ 555-1992
   Ⓑ 555-1979
   Ⓒ 555-2000

6. Her birthday is in _____.
   Ⓐ Brazil
   Ⓑ September
   Ⓒ October

Check your answers. See page 132.

2 Circle the words.

1. country   c o (c o u n t r y) t e
2. name   m e n a m e a n
3. June   l J u l J u n e J y
4. month   m o n m o n t h t h
5. birthday   d a y b i r t h d a y b i
6. phone   p h p h o n e p n

3 What is different? Cross it out.

1.	Brazil	China	~~August~~	Mexico
2.	470	555-9832	212	201
3.	555-6782	555-1508	555-3744	972
4.	March	Somalia	October	July
5.	Vladimir	William	Russia	Rachel
6.	China	January	Mexico	Somalia
7.	May	September	December	Brazil

4 Number the months in the correct order.

_1_ January   ___ December
___ April   ___ March
___ August   ___ February
___ July   ___ October
___ May   ___ September
___ November   ___ June

January

Sunday	Monday	Tuesday	Wednesday	Thursday	Friday	Saturday
		1	2	3	4	5	6
7	8	9	10	11	12	13
14	15	16	17	18	19	20
21	22	23	24	25	26	27
28	29	30	31			

LESSON **A** Listening

1 Look at the pictures. Match.

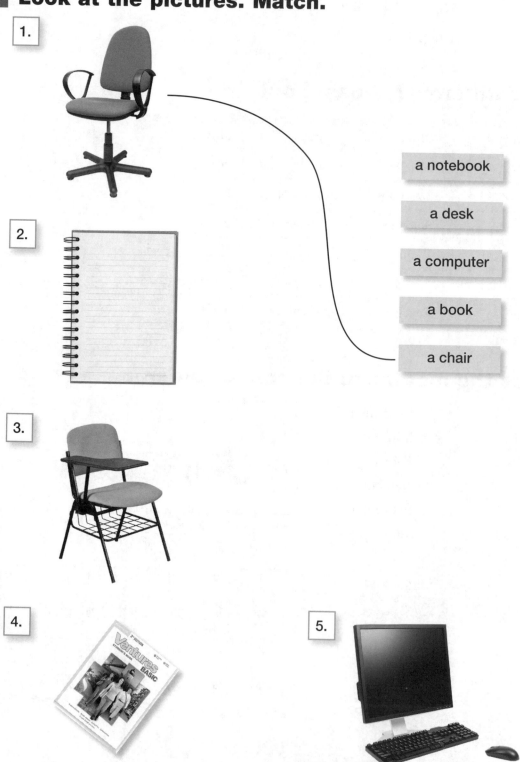

1.

2.

3.

4.

5.

a notebook

a desk

a computer

a book

a chair

Check your answers. See page 132.

2 Listen and number.

TRACK 6

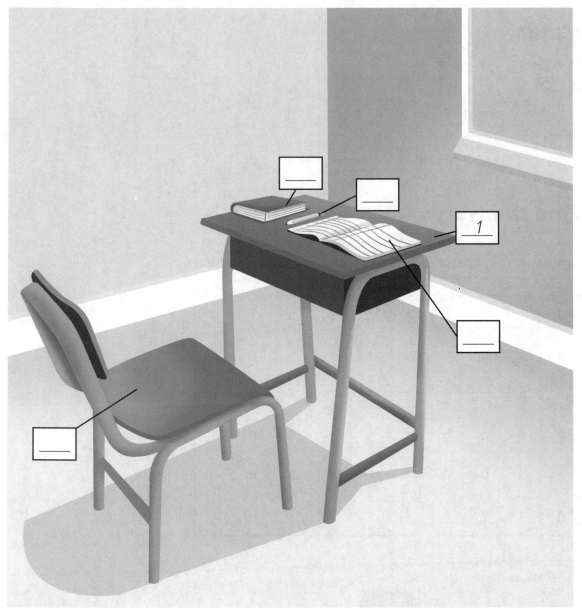

3 Complete the words.

1. b o o _k_

2. n o t e b o o ___

3. d e s ___

4. ___ o m p u t e r

5. p e n ___ i l

6. ___ h a i r

Check your answers. See page 132.

LESSON **B** Classroom objects

1 Match.

1. sta
2. rul
3. dictio
4. era
5. pa

ser
per
er
pler
nary

2 Find the words.

| dictionary | eraser | paper | pen | ruler | stapler |

d	i	c	t	i	o	n	a	r	y
p	i	d	d	e	r	a	s	e	r
l	a	e	s	t	a	p	l	e	r
p	a	p	e	r	b	v	z	p	x
w	s	b	a	l	o	y	p	e	n
q	u	y	s	f	r	u	l	e	r

Check your answers. See page 132.

3 Complete the words.

dictionary	eraser	paper	pen	ruler	stapler

1. d <u>_i_</u> <u>_c_</u> <u>_t_</u> <u>_i_</u> <u>_o_</u> <u>_n_</u> <u>_a_</u> <u>_r_</u> <u>_y_</u>
2. p ___ ___ ___
3. p ___ ___
4. r ___ ___ ___ ___
5. s ___ ___ ___ ___ ___ ___
6. e ___ ___ ___ ___ ___

4 Look at the pictures. Write the words.

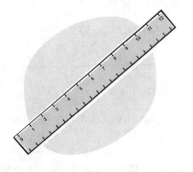

1. a _____

2. a _____

3. an _____

4. a _____

5. a _____

6. _____

LESSON C Where's my pencil?

1 **Look at the picture. Match. Write the letter.**

1. __c__ pencil   a. on the desk

2. _____ eraser   b. under the desk

3. _____ paper   c. in the desk

4. _____ dictionary   d. on the chair

5. _____ notebook   e. on the notebook

2 **Look at the picture in Exercise 1. Write *in*, *on*, or *under*. Then listen.**

TRACK 7

1. Where's my pencil?   ____*In*____ the desk.

2. Where's my notebook?   _____ the chair.

3. Where's my dictionary?   _____ the desk.

4. Where's my paper?   _____ the desk.

5. Where's my eraser?   _____ the notebook.

Check your answers. See page 132.

3 **Look at the picture. Write the answers. Then listen.**

TRACK 8

1. *A* Where's my dictionary?

   B _____ *On the desk* _____.

2. *A* Where's my pencil?

   B _____.

3. *A* Where's my eraser?

   B _____.

4. *A* Where's my paper?

   B _____.

5. *A* Where's my notebook?

   B _____.

6. *A* Where's my ruler?

   B _____.

Check your answers. See page 132.

LESSON D Reading

1 Circle the words.

1. notebook   n o t n o t e b o o k t e
2. eraser   e r e r a s e r a s
3. computer   c c o m p u t e r t e r
4. pencil   e n p e n c i l i l p
5. desk   e s k d e s k d e n c i l
6. book   k o b o o o k b o o k

2 Read. Circle the correct sentences. Then listen.

TRACK 9

> *Dear Students,*
>
> *Welcome to English class!*
> * *You need a pencil.*
> * *You need an eraser.*
> * *You need a notebook.*
> * *You need a dictionary.*
> * *You need a ruler.*
>
> *Thank you.*
>
> *Your teacher,*
> *Ellen*

SCHOOL CENTER AVENUE ADULT

1. You need a dictionary.   You need a chair.
2. You need paper.   You need a pencil.
3. You need a computer.   You need a notebook.
4. You need a ruler.   You need a stapler.
5. You need an eraser.   You need a pen.

Check your answers. See pages 132–133.

3 Number the days in the correct order.

_1_ Sunday   ____ Thursday

____ Friday   ____ Tuesday

____ Monday   ____ Saturday

____ Wednesday

4 Write the words.

| Friday | Monday | Sunday | Thursday | Tuesday | Wednesday |

```
                        S  u   n   d   a   y
        M  ___ ___ ___  a  ___
                        t
                   ___  u  ___ ___ ___ ___
                   ___  r  ___ ___ ___ ___
              ___ ___    d  ___ ___ ___ ___ ___
                        a
        T  ___ ___ ___ ___ ___ ___  y
```

5 Write the days of the week.

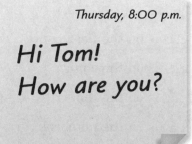

1. **A** What day is it?

   B _____ Friday _____ .

2. **A** What day is it?

   B _____ .

3. **A** What day is it?

   B _____ .

Check your answers. See page 133.

1 **Look at the picture. Complete the sentences.**

| dictionary | eraser | notebook | pencil | ruler | stapler |

1. The _____notebook_____ is on the floor.

2. The _____ is on the chair.

3. The _____ is on the table.

4. The _____ is on the notebook.

5. The _____ is in the notebook.

6. The _____ is under the chair.

Check your answers. See page 133.

2 Look at the picture. Write *in*, *on*, or *under*.

What a mess! The dictionary is _____*on*_____ the chair. The stapler
1
is _____ the dictionary. The eraser is _____ the desk.
2   3
The pencil is _____ the desk. The notebook is _____ the desk.
4   5
The ruler is _____ the notebook.
6

3 Unscramble the letters. Match.

1. c i p e l n ──────── ruler

2. r a e r s e   notebook

3. u l r e r   dictionary

4. a p p r e ────────── pencil

5. a r y d t c i o i n   eraser

6. t o o b k e n o   paper

4 Write the words from Exercise 3.

School Supplies for Class

1. I need a _____*pencil*_____.

2. I need an _____.

3. I need a _____.

4. I need _____.

5. I need a _____.

6. I need a _____.

Check your answers. See page 133.

LESSON F Another view

1 Read the sentences. Look at the class schedule. Fill in the correct answers.

Red Rock Adult School Classes

Monday	Tuesday	Wednesday	Thursday
Computers	English	Computers	English
7:00–8:30 p.m.	6:30–8:00 p.m.	7:00–8:30 p.m.	6:30–8:00 p.m.

Computer Teacher:
Sheila Brown
Room: 106

English Teacher:
Brad Ryan
Room: 217

1. The English class is on ____.
   Ⓐ Monday and Tuesday
   Ⓑ Monday and Thursday
   ● Tuesday and Thursday

2. The computer class is on ____.
   Ⓐ Tuesday and Wednesday
   Ⓑ Monday and Wednesday
   Ⓒ Monday and Thursday

3. The computer class is in ____.
   Ⓐ Room 106
   Ⓑ Room 700
   Ⓒ Room 217

4. The teacher on Monday and Wednesday is ____.
   Ⓐ Brad Brown
   Ⓑ Brad Ryan
   Ⓒ Sheila Brown

5. The teacher on Tuesday and Thursday is ____.
   Ⓐ Brad Ryan
   Ⓑ Sheila Brown
   Ⓒ Sheila Ryan

6. The English class is in ____.
   Ⓐ Room 630
   Ⓑ Room 217
   Ⓒ Room 106

Check your answers. See page 133.

2 Complete the puzzle.

| desk | dictionary | eraser | notebook | pen | pencil | ruler | stapler |

Across →

1.

4.

5.

7.

8.

Down ↓

2.

3.

6.

1 p	e	2 n					3	
4								
			5					
							6	
			7					
8								

UNIT 3 Friends and family

LESSON **A** Listening

1 **Look at the pictures. Circle the correct words.**

1.

son (grandmother)

2.

daughter   son

3.

grandfather   daughter

4.

father   mother

5.

father   grandmother

6.

mother   son

2 **Complete the words.**

1. s __o__ n

2. f ____ t h ____ r

3. m ____ t h ____ r

4. g r ____ n d m ____ t h ____ r

5. d ____ ____ g h t ____ r

6. g r ____ n d f ____ t h ____ r

Check your answers. See page 133.

3 Listen and number the picture.

TRACK 10

4 Look at the picture in Exercise 3. Write the words.

1. _m_ _o_ _t_ _h_ _e_ _r_
2. ___ ___ ___ ___ ___ ___
3. ___ ___ ___ ___ ___ ___ ___ ___
4. ___ ___ ___
5. ___ ___ ___ ___ ___ ___ ___ ___ ___ ___
6. ___ ___ ___ ___ ___ ___ ___ ___ ___ ___

Check your answers. See page 133.

LESSON **B** Family members

1 Match.

1. sister ———— daughter
2. son — uncle
3. grandmother —— brother
4. husband — father
5. mother — grandfather
6. aunt — wife

2 Write the words.

| aunt | brother | husband | sister | wife |

```
                    m
    _b_ _r_ o _t_ _h_ _e_ _r_
    ___ ___ ___   t
                  h   __ __ __ __ __
    ___ ___ ___   e
                  r
__ __ __ __ __
```

Check your answers. See page 133.

3 **Circle the correct letters.**

1. aunt and uncle   (a.)

Anita   Rick

b.

Michael   Emily

2. mother and father   a.

Julie   Jason

b.

Michael   Emily

3. brother and sister   a.

Julie   Jason

b.

Michael   Emily

4 **Look at the pictures in Exercise 3. Write the answers.**

1. **A** Who is Michael?

   B Emily's ___brother___ .

2. **A** Who is Emily?

   B Michael's _____ .

3. **A** Who is Jason?

   B Michael's _____ .

4. **A** Who is Julie?

   B Michael's _____ .

5. **A** Who is Rick?

   B Michael's _____ .

6. **A** Who is Anita?

   B Emily's _____ .

LESSON C Do you have a sister?

Study the chart on page 128.

1 **Look at the pictures. Circle the answers. Then write.**

1. **A** Do you have a son?

   B ___No, we don't.___
   Yes, we do. (No, we don't.)

2. **A** Do you have a brother?

   B _____
   Yes, I do.   No, I don't.

3. **A** Do you have a daughter?

   B _____
   Yes, we do.   No, we don't.

4. **A** Do you have a wife?

   B _____
   Yes, I do.   No, I don't.

5. **A** Do you have a grandmother?

   B _____
   Yes, I do.   No, I don't.

Check your answers. See page 133.

2 Look and listen. Then write the answers.

TRACK 11

| daughter | husband | sister | son |

1. **A** Carla, do you have a _____*sister*_____?

   B Yes, I do.

   A What's her name?

   B Gabriela.

2. **A** Carla, do you have a _____?

   B Yes, I do.

   A What's her name?

   B Inez.

3. **A** Carla, do you have a _____?

   B Yes, I do.

   A What's his name?

   B Roberto.

4. **A** Carla, do you have a _____?

   B Yes, I do.

   A What's his name?

   B Alfredo.

Check your answers. See page 133.   **UNIT 3** **35**

LESSON D Reading

1 Read. Write the words. Then listen.

TRACK 12

My Family

My name is Geraldo. This is my family. This is my father. His name is Hugo. This is my mother. Her name is Magdalena. This is my wife, Pilar. This is my daughter, Ramona.

daughter   father   mother   wife

Geraldo

1. _____wife_____

2. _____

3. _____

4. _____

Pilar   Ramona   Hugo   Magdalena

2 Look at the story in Exercise 1. Circle the answers.

1. Ramona is Geraldo's mother.   Yes   (No)

2. Pilar is Geraldo's wife.   Yes   No

3. Magdalena is Geraldo's mother.   Yes   No

4. Hugo is Geraldo's brother.   Yes   No

5. Ramona is Hugo's wife.   Yes   No

Check your answers. See page 134.

3 **Complete the chart.**

baby	boy	girl	man	teenager	woman

Male	Female	Male or Female
boy		

4 **Circle the answers. Then write the answers.**

1. Pat is a mother. Pat is a _____ woman _____.
   man (woman)

2. Joe is a father. Joe is a _____.
   man   woman

3. Charles is a son. Charles is a _____.
   boy   girl

4. Debbie is a daughter. Debbie is a _____.
   boy   girl

5. Sharon is a wife. Sharon is a _____.
   man   woman

6. Jimmy is a husband. Jimmy is a _____.
   man   woman

7. Nancy is a grandmother. Nancy is a _____.
   man   woman

8. Heather is 13 years old. Heather is a _____.
   teenager   baby

9. Mark is one year old. Mark is a _____.
   teenager   baby

LESSON E Writing

1 **Unscramble the letters. Write the words.**

| daughter | grandfather | mother | sister | uncle | wife |

1. i f w e   _____*wife*_____

2. n u l e c   _____

3. s s i e t r   _____

4. o e m h t r   _____

5. d t h r e g a u   _____

6. g f r a t a d n r h e   _____

2 **Write. Use the words from Exercise 1.**

1. aunt and _____*uncle*_____

2. brother and _____

3. son and _____

4. husband and _____

5. father and _____

6. grandmother and _____

3 **Look at the baby's family. Write the words.**

1. _____

2. _____

3. _____*baby*_____

4. _____

5. _____

Check your answers. See page 134.

4 **Look at Viktor's family. Write the words.**

brother	daughter	father	mother	son	wife

Greg
1. ___*father*___

Irina
2. _____

Boris
3. _____

Viktor

Sylvia
4. _____

Arthur
5. _____

Olivia
6. _____

5 **Look at the picture in Exercise 4. Complete the sentences.**

1. Viktor is Sylvia's ___*husband*___ .

2. Viktor is Irina's _____ .

3. Viktor is Arthur's _____ .

4. Viktor is Greg's _____ .

5. Viktor is Boris's _____ .

6. Viktor is Olivia's _____ .

Check your answers. See page 134.   UNIT 3 **39**

1 **Read the questions. Look at the form. Fill in the correct answers.**

Census Form		
Name: Tia Sanchez		
Address: 333 Main Street		
City: San Antonio	**State:** TX	**Zip Code:** 78205
Who lives with you in your house?		
First name	**Last name**	**Relation**
1. Raul	Gonzalez	father
2. Consuela	Gonzalez	mother
3. Roberto	Sanchez	husband
4. Rodrigo	Sanchez	son
5. Pedro	Sanchez	son
6. Lara	Sanchez	daughter

1. Who is Lara Sanchez?
   Ⓐ Tia's mother
   ● Tia's daughter
   © Tia's son

2. Who is Roberto Sanchez?
   Ⓐ Tia's father
   Ⓑ Tia's husband
   © Tia's son

3. Who is Pedro Sanchez?
   Ⓐ Tia's father
   Ⓑ Tia's husband
   © Tia's son

4. Who is Consuela Gonzalez?
   Ⓐ Tia's mother
   Ⓑ Tia's daughter
   © Tia's father

5. Who is Raul Gonzalez?
   Ⓐ Tia's father
   Ⓑ Tia's husband
   © Tia's son

6. Who is Tia Sanchez?
   Ⓐ Roberto's mother
   Ⓑ Roberto's daughter
   © Roberto's wife

Check your answers. See page 134.

2 What is different? Cross it out.

1.	aunt	woman	~~father~~	wife
2.	grandfather	son	husband	aunt
3.	daughter	son	wife	grandmother
4.	brother	uncle	aunt	man
5.	mother	brother	grandmother	daughter
6.	father	boy	grandfather	wife
7.	girl	man	aunt	woman

3 Find the words.

baby	mother	teenager	wife
husband	sister	uncle	woman

w	i	f	e	o	r	d	i	m	b	a	b	y	g
o	w	o	m	a	n	r	s	i	s	t	r	v	e
s	i	s	t	e	r	s	t	f	l	c	e	l	o
c	a	m	e	r	t	m	o	t	h	e	r	n	k
h	u	s	b	a	n	d	s	h	o	u	m	k	l
n	m	o	w	i	e	t	e	e	n	a	g	e	r
u	n	c	l	e	t	b	u	b	f	w	a	p	o

Check your answers. See page 134.

LESSON **A** Listening

1 **Look at the pictures. Circle the correct words.**

1.

~~patient~~ (circled)
nurse
doctor

2.

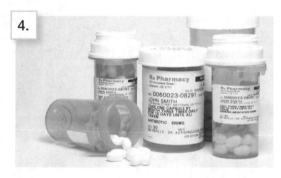

nurse
doctor's office
doctor

3.

medicine
patient
nurse

4.

doctor
nurse
medicine

5.

medicine
doctor
patient

6.

doctor's office
nurse
patient

Check your answers. See page 134.

2 Listen and number.

TRACK 13

3 Look at the picture in Exercise 2. Unscramble the letters.

1. 'srtdoco cfofei _____

2. snreu _____

3. tanipet _____

4. emdcneii _____

5. rodtco _____

LESSON B Parts of the body

1 **Complete the words.**

1. h __a__ n d

2. h e ____ d

3. f ____ o t

4. ____ r m

5. l ____ g

6. s t o m ____ c h

2 **Look at the pictures. What hurts? Write the words from Exercise 1.**

1. My ___stomach___!

2. My _____!

3. My _____!

4. My _____!

5. My _____!

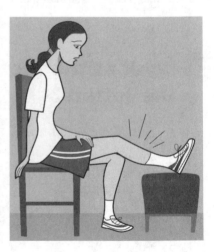

6. My _____!

Check your answers. See page 134.

3 Look at the pictures. Complete the sentences. Then listen.

TRACK 14

1. **A** What's the matter?

   B My ___foot___ hurts.

2. **A** What's the matter?

   B My _____ hurts.

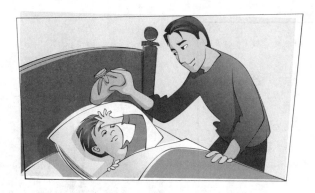

3. **A** What's the matter?

   B My _____ hurts.

4. **A** What's the matter?

   B My _____ hurts.

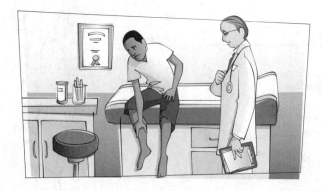

5. **A** What's the matter?

   B My _____ hurts.

6. **A** What's the matter?

   B My _____ hurts.

Check your answers. See page 134.

LESSON C My feet hurt.

1 Match.

1. eye ⎯⎯⎯⎯⎯ feet
2. hand ⎯⎯⎯⎯ arms
3. foot ⎯⎯⎯⎯ eyes
4. arm hands
5. leg legs

2 Find the words.

arms	eyes	feet	foot	hands	head	legs

r	e	p	l	e	g	s	t	u	r
f	q	b	o	p	h	a	n	d	s
o	u	m	j	f	e	e	t	k	e
f	o	o	t	t	l	s	c	z	j
t	e	r	h	e	a	d	z	y	e
a	r	m	s	c	o	m	u	t	r
l	e	k	f	t	p	e	y	e	s

Check your answers. See page 134.

3 Look at the pictures. Complete the chart.

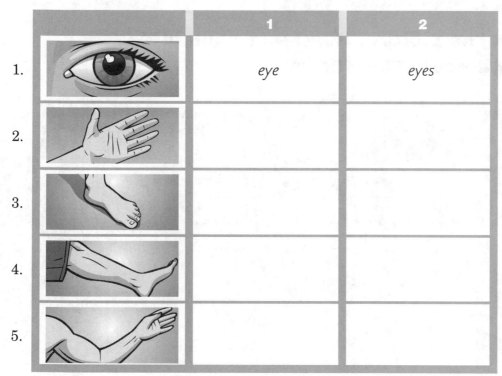

		1	2
1.		*eye*	*eyes*
2.			
3.			
4.			
5.			

4 Look at the pictures. Write the words.

1. **A** What hurts?

   B My ___*legs*___ !

2. **A** What hurts?

   B My _____ !

3. **A** What hurts?

   B My _____ !

4. **A** What hurts?

   B My _____ !

5. **A** What hurts?

   B My _____ !

6. **A** What hurts?

   B My _____ !

Check your answers. See pages 134–135.

LESSON D Reading

1 Look at the picture. Read and complete the sentences. Then listen.

TRACK 15

Where's the Doctor?

Five patients are at the doctor's office. The nurse is talking to the patients. Ruth's stomach hurts. Jun's arm hurts. Liliana's leg hurts. Omar's hand hurts. Tano's foot hurts. Where's the doctor? Doctor Han is not in his office. His head hurts. He is home in bed.

1. *Nurse* What hurts?

   Ruth My ___stomach___ hurts.

2. *Nurse* What hurts?

   Omar My _____ hurts.

3. *Nurse* What hurts?

   Tano My _____ hurts.

4. *Nurse* What hurts?

   Jun My _____ hurts.

5. *Nurse* What hurts?

   Liliana My _____ hurts.

6. *Nurse* What hurts?

   Doctor My _____ hurts.

Check your answers. See page 135.

2 Look at the picture. Match. Write the letter.

1. __c__ Ms. Simon   a. a cold
2. ____ Matt   b. a fever
3. ____ Ella   c. a headache
4. ____ Stefano   d. a sore throat
5. ____ Reyna   e. a stomachache
6. ____ Minh   f. a toothache

3 Look at the pictures. Complete the sentences.

1. I have a __toothache__.   2. I have a _____.   3. I have a _____.

LESSON E Writing

1 Complete the puzzle.

arm	eyes	legs	stomachache
cold	headache	sore throat	toothache

Across →

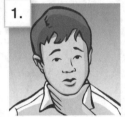 1.

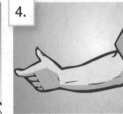 4.

 5.

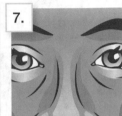 7.

Down ↓

 1.

 2.

 3.

 6.

4. a r m

Check your answers. See page 135.

2 Unscramble the letters. Write the words.

cold   headache   fever   sore throat   stomachache

1. c l d o   _____cold_____

2. v r e e f   _____

3. d c h e a a e h _____

4. o m a c s t h c e h a _____

5. o r s e   o h r t a t _____

3 Read. Complete the sentences.

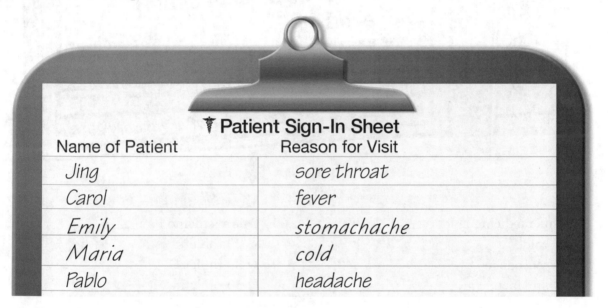

⚕ Patient Sign-In Sheet

Name of Patient	Reason for Visit
Jing	sore throat
Carol	fever
Emily	stomachache
Maria	cold
Pablo	headache

1. Jing   I have a ____sore throat____ .

2. Maria   I have a _____ .

3. Pablo   I have a _____ .

4. Emily   I have a _____ .

5. Carol   I have a _____ .

LESSON F Another view

1 **Read the sentences. Look at the label. Fill in the correct answers.**

1. This medicine is for a _____.
   ● cold
   Ⓑ toothache
   Ⓒ stomachache

2. This medicine is for a _____.
   Ⓐ headache
   Ⓑ fever
   Ⓒ toothache

3. This medicine is for a _____.
   Ⓐ stomachache
   Ⓑ sore throat
   Ⓒ headache

4. Do not take this medicine _____.
   Ⓐ after January 2013
   Ⓑ after January 2014
   Ⓒ after January 2015

5. This medicine has _____.
   Ⓐ 20 tablets
   Ⓑ 30 tablets
   Ⓒ 50 tablets

6. This medicine is not for _____.
   Ⓐ toothaches
   Ⓑ fevers
   Ⓒ colds

Check your answers. See page 135.

2 **Look at the picture. Write the words.**

1. _hands_
2. _____
3. _____
4. _____
5. _____

3 **What hurts? Look at the picture. Complete the sentences.**

1. _____My head_____ hurts!

2. _____ hurts!

3. _____ hurts!

4. _____ hurts!

Check your answers. See page 135.

LESSON **A** Listening

1 **Look at the pictures. Match.**

restaurant

library

school

supermarket

bank

Check your answers. See page 135.

2 Listen and number.

TRACK 16

a. _____

d. _____

b. _____

e. _____

c. _____

3 Unscramble the letters. Write the words.

| bank | restaurant | street |
| library | school | supermarket |

1. s r e t e t _____*street*_____

2. k a b n _____

3. h c s l o o _____

4. b l i r r a y _____

5. t a u n r a t e s r _____

6. m k t a r e p e r u s _____

LESSON B Places around town

1 Match. Then write the words.

1. phar ———— station   _____
2. movie ————— macy   _____*pharmacy*_____
3. gas   office   _____
4. post   tal   _____
5. laundro   mat   _____
6. hospi   theater   _____

2 Find the words.

gas station	laundromat	pharmacy
hospital	movie theater	post office

t	w	j	v	e	a	x	p	b	u	o	y	g	z
x	c	j	b	v	g	o	v	x	j	m	p	b	m
p	o	s	t	o	f	f	i	c	e	l	u	j	j
g	a	s	s	t	a	t	i	o	n	y	h	a	a
u	x	c	o	u	j	m	q	h	o	s	p	a	w
g	p	u	a	l	a	u	n	d	r	o	m	a	t
p	h	a	r	m	a	c	y	l	r	p	m	q	s
r	s	o	f	v	a	k	p	o	l	h	d	f	t
m	o	v	i	e	t	h	e	a	t	e	r	g	u
h	j	p	e	d	y	h	o	s	p	i	t	a	l
a	l	a	u	n	d	p	n	g	e	i	o	c	e

Check your answers. See page 135.

3 Look at the pictures. Write the answers.

gas station	laundromat	pharmacy
hospital	movie theater	post office

1. **A** Where's Mark?

   B At the _____hospital_____.

2. **A** Where's Maya?

   B At the _____.

3. **A** Where's Jane?

   B At the _____.

4. **A** Where's Pavel?

   B At the _____.

5. **A** Where's Claudia?

   B At the _____.

6. **A** Where's Peter?

   B At the _____.

Check your answers. See page 135.

1 **Look at the picture. Circle the answers. Then write.**

1. The pharmacy is _____*next to*_____ the supermarket.
   (next to) across from

2. The school is _____ the library.
   next to   across from

3. The supermarket is _____ the post office.
   next to   across from

4. The post office is _____ Main Street.
   on   across from

5. The bank is _____ the restaurant and the movie theater.
   across from   between

6. The restaurant is _____ the post office.
   between   across from

7. The library is _____ the post office.
   across from   at

8. The supermarket is _____ the pharmacy and the post office.
   across from   between

Check your answers. See page 135.

2 Look at the map. Write the words.

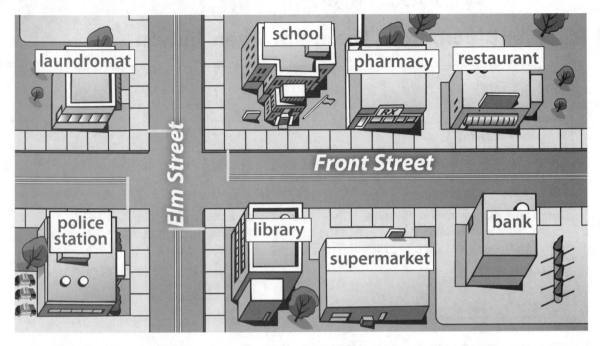

Across from	Between	Next to	On

1. **A** Where's the restaurant?

   B _____ Next to _____ the pharmacy.

2. **A** Where's the school?

   B _____ the library.

3. **A** Where's the pharmacy?

   B _____ the school and the restaurant.

4. **A** Where's the restaurant?

   B _____ Front Street.

3 Look at the map in Exercise 2. Match. Write the letter.

1. __c__ the laundromat   a. next to the pharmacy

2. ____ the supermarket   b. across from the laundromat

3. ____ the school   c. on Elm Street

4. ____ the library   d. between the library and the bank

5. ____ the police station   e. across from the school

LESSON D Reading

TRACK 17

1 Read and complete the map. Then listen.

Reply   Delete   Forward

From: ming@cup.org
To: carey@cup.org
Re: New Restaurant

Dear Carey,

Come and visit my new restaurant! The restaurant is on Lake Street. It is across from the hospital. It is between the bank and the pharmacy. It is open from 11:00 a.m. to 11:00 p.m., Monday to Saturday. Here is a map.

Best wishes,
Ming

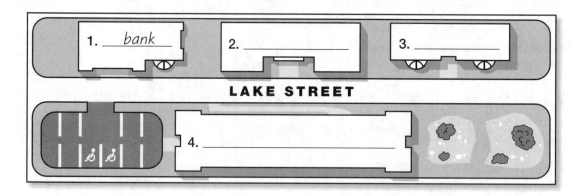

1. _bank_   2. _____   3. _____

LAKE STREET

4. _____

2 Look at the map in Exercise 1. Listen and write the words.

TRACK 18

1. *A* Where's the restaurant?

   B Across from the _____ *hospital* _____.

2. *A* Where's the restaurant?

   B On _____.

3. *A* Where's the restaurant?

   B Between the _____ and the _____.

4. *A* Where's the bank?

   B Next to the _____.

Check your answers. See pages 135–136.

3 Complete the words.

bicycle	bus	car	foot	taxi	train

1. by c _a_ _r_

2. by t ___ ___ ___

3. by b ___ ___ ___ ___ ___ ___

4. by b ___ ___

5. by t ___ ___ ___ ___

6. on f ___ ___ ___

4 Look at the picture. Complete the chart.

Name	Transportation
Yoko	by taxi
Ted	
Martin	
Nadia	
Sam	
Katia	

Check your answers. See page 136.

LESSON E Writing

1 **Look at the map. Write the words.**

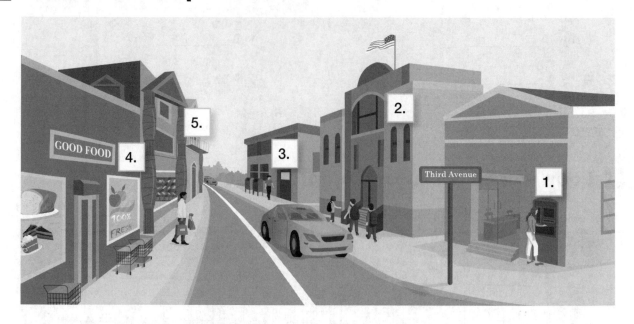

| bank | library | post office | school | supermarket |

1. _____bank_____   4. _____

2. _____   5. _____

3. _____

2 **Look at the map in Exercise 1. Complete the sentences.**

> ### *City School*
>
> The City School is on _____*Third Avenue*_____ . It is
>   1
> across from a _____ . The school is between
>   2
> the _____ and the _____ .
>   3   4
> A _____ is on Third Avenue, too.
>   5

Check your answers. See page 136.

3 **Look at the map. Complete the sentences.**

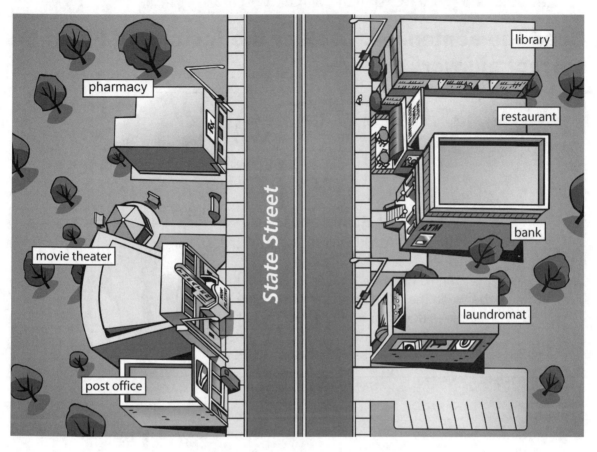

| across from | between | on | next to | across from | on |

State Street Movie Theater

The movie theater is _____*on*_____ State Street.

1

It is _____ a post office. A laundromat is

2

_____ the movie theater.

3

Dave's Family Restaurant is _____ State Street, too.

4

It is _____ the library and the bank. The restaurant is

5

_____ the pharmacy. See you at the movies!

6

Check your answers. See page 136.

LESSON F Another view

1 **Read the sentences. Look at the invitation. Fill in the correct answers.**

COME TO A PARTY

Where? At Binh's house
When? At 8:00 p.m. on Saturday

Binh's house is on Center Street. It is between the library and the post office. Binh's house is across from the supermarket. There is a movie theater next to the supermarket, too. The address is 259 Center Street.

1. Binh's house is _____.
   ● on Center Street
   ⑧ on Post Street
   ⓒ on Market Street

2. Binh's house is _____.
   Ⓐ between the supermarket and the post office
   ⑧ between the library and the post office
   ⓒ between the movie theater and the supermarket

3. The supermarket is _____.
   Ⓐ next to Binh's house
   ⑧ next to the post office
   ⓒ across from Binh's house

4. The library is _____.
   Ⓐ next to the post office
   ⑧ next to Binh's house
   ⓒ next to the supermarket

5. The movie theater is _____.
   Ⓐ next to the supermarket
   ⑧ across from the supermarket
   ⓒ next to Binh's house

6. The post office is _____.
   Ⓐ across from the movie theater
   ⑧ next to the supermarket
   ⓒ between the library and Binh's house

Check your answers. See page 136.

2 | Circle the words.

1. bus   b a n k ⊂b u s⊃ s t r e e t c a r

2. taxi   t r a i n f o o t t a x i b a n k

3. train   t a x i b u s c e n t e r t r a i n

4. bicycle   l i b r a r y b i c y c l e f o o t

5. foot   c a r a c r o s s f o o t t a x i

6. car   s h o p c a r s t o r e p o s t

3 | Listen and read. Complete the conversations.

TRACK 19

| Excuse me   Next to the pharmacy   Thanks   Where's the supermarket |

1. **A** _____ *Excuse me* _____ . Where's the laundromat?

   B On Maple Street.

   A Thanks.

2. **A** Excuse me. Where's the movie theater?

   B Across from Rosa's Restaurant.

   A _____ .

3. **A** Excuse me. _____ ?

   B Between the bank and the library.

   A Thanks.

4. **A** Excuse me. Where's the bank?

   B _____ .

   A Thanks.

LESSON **A** Listening

1 Match.

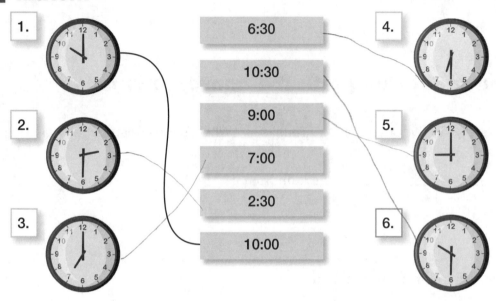

1. 🕐
2. 🕑
3. 🕓

6:30
10:30
9:00
7:00
2:30
10:00

4. 🕐
5. 🕘
6. 🕗

2 Read. Write the time.

TIME CARD		
DAY	**DATE**	**TIME IN**
Monday	May 12	2:30

1. _____2:30_____

TIME CARD		
DAY	**DATE**	**TIME IN**
Thursday	March 3	9:00

2. _____9:00_____

TIME CARD		
DAY	**DATE**	**TIME IN**
Saturday	June 21	10:30

3. _____10:30_____

TIME CARD		
DAY	**DATE**	**TIME IN**
Tuesday	July 8	7:00

4. _____7:00_____

Check your answers. See page 136.

3 **Listen and draw the hands on the clocks.**

TRACK 20

1.

2.

3.

4.

5.

6.

7.

8.

9.

Check your answers. See page 136.

LESSON B Events

1 Read. Write the answers.

Monday

4:30 appointment
with Dr. Jones

MARCH 17

1. **A** What time is the appointment?
   B At ____4:30____ on ____Monday____.

Tuesday

3:30 meeting with
Dr. Kwan

MARCH 18

2. **A** What time is the meeting?
   B At ____3:30____ on ____Tuesday____.

Wednesday

9:30 movie with
Paco

MARCH 19

3. **A** What time is the movie?
   B At ____9:30____ on ____Wednesday____.

Thursday

5:00 class

MARCH 20

4. **A** What time is the class?
   B At ____5:00____ on ____Thursday____.

2 Complete the words.

appointment	class	meeting	movie	party	show

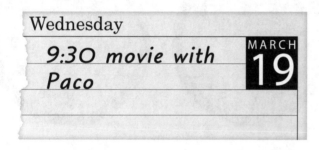

1. c __l__ __a__ __s__ __s__

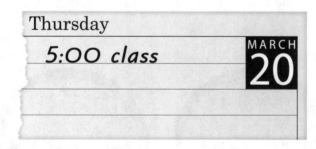

2. m __o__ __v__ __i__ __e__

3. p __a__ __r__ __t__ __y__

4. m __e__ __e__ __t__ __i__ __n__ __g__

5. a __p__ __p__ __o__ __i__ __n__ __t__ __m__ __e__ __n__ __t__

6. TV s __h__ __o__ __w__

Check your answers. See page 136.

3 **Look at the pictures. Write the words.**

| appointment | class | meeting | movie | party | TV show |

1. **A** What time is the ____meeting____?
   B At ____10:00____ .

2. **A** What time is the ____party____?
   B At ____8:30____ .

3. **A** What time is the ____class____?
   B At ____11:00____ .

4. **A** What time is the ____appointment____?
   B At ____3:30____ .

JACK AND JANE
7:30

5. **A** What time is the ____movie____?
   B At ____7:30____ .

6. **A** What time is the ____TV show____?
   B At ____9:00____ .

Check your answers. See page 136.

LESSON C Is your class at 11:00?

Study the chart on page 126.

1 Look at the pictures. Write the answers.

From: walker@cup.org

To: jones@cup.org

Dear Employees:

Our meeting is today at 11:00 a.m.

1. **A** Is the meeting at 12:00?

   B <u>No, it isn't. It's at 11:00 a.m.</u>

ADMIT ONE
Love at Sunset
7:45 p.m.   Sat. 8/9/08
Theater 2

2. **A** Is the movie at 8:00?

   B <u>No, it isn't. It's at 7:45pm</u>

PARTY TONIGHT!
The Jam Club
Free Admission
8:30 p.m.

3. **A** Is the party at 8:30?

   B <u>Yes, it is</u>

CITY LIGHTS
Orchestra
JULY **19** SAT.
Seat K32
8:00 p.m.

4. **A** Is the concert at 6:30?

   B <u>No, it isn't. It's at 8:00pm</u>

Appointment Card

Your appointment:
3:30 p.m.
September 12

5. **A** Is the appointment at 3:30?

   B <u>Yes, it is</u>

Check your answers. See page 136.

2 Look and read. Circle the correct answers. Then listen.

TRACK 21

Monday, September 15			
8:30	Class	4:00	
9:00		5:00	Doctor's appointment 😧
10:00		6:30	
11:00		7:00	Movie with Louis
12:00	Lunch with Don 🙂	8:00	
1:00		9:00	Birthday party 🙂
2:00		10:00	
3:00	Meeting at work 😧	11:00	

1. Is the class at 8:00? Yes, it is. (No, it isn't.)

2. Is the appointment at 3:00? Yes, it is. (No, it isn't.)

3. Is the party at 9:00? (Yes, it is.) No, it isn't.

4. Is the movie at 6:30? Yes, it is. (No, it isn't.)

5. Is the meeting at 3:00? (Yes, it is.) No, it isn't.

3 Look at the information in Exercise 2. Match.

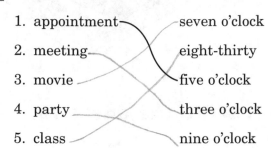

1. appointment   seven o'clock
2. meeting   eight-thirty
3. movie   five o'clock
4. party   three o'clock
5. class   nine o'clock

Check your answers. See pages 136–137.   UNIT 6   **71**

LESSON **D** Reading

1 **Read and number the sentences in the correct order. Then listen.**

Mahmoud's Day

Mahmoud is busy today. His favorite TV show is at 7:30 in the morning. His doctor's appointment is at 10:30. His meeting with Abram is at 12:00. His English class is at 1:00 in the afternoon. His concert is at 5:00. His sister's birthday party is at 8:00 in the evening. What a day!

FROM THE DESK OF YOUR DOCTOR:

YOUR APPOINTMENT IS AT:
10:30 A.M.

ADMIT ONE
LIVE Jazz
5:00 P.M.
SEAT 42C

LIVE JAZZ
5:00 P.M. SEAT 42C
ADMIT ONE

___6___ his sister's birthday party.

___2___ his doctor's appointment.

___1___ his favorite TV show.

___5___ his concert.

___4___ his English class.

___3___ his meeting with Abram.

2 **Look at the story in Exercise 1. Write the answers.**

1. What time is Mahmoud's appointment? _____At 10:30_____.

2. What time is Mahmoud's meeting with Abram? _____at 12:00 pm_____.

3. What time is Mahmoud's English class? _____at 1:00 pm_____.

4. What time is Mahmoud's favorite TV show? _____at 7:30_____.

5. What time is Mahmoud's concert? _____at 5:00 pm_____

6. What time is his sister's birthday party? _____at 8:00 pm_____.

Check your answers. See page 137.

3 Match.

a. in the evening   b. in the morning   c. at night   d. in the afternoon

4 Match. Write the letter.

1. __d__ 8:00 a.m.
2. __e__ 12:00 p.m.
3. __b__ 3:30 p.m.
4. __f__ 12:00 a.m.
5. __a__ 7:30 p.m.
6. __a__ 11:00 p.m.

a. in the evening
b. in the afternoon
c. at night
d. in the morning
e. at noon
f. at midnight

5 Write the words.

at midnight	at noon	in the evening
at night	in the afternoon	in the morning

1. 6:30 a.m. _____in the morning_____
2. 2:00 p.m. _____in the afternoon_____
3. 10:30 p.m. _____at night_____
4. 12:00 p.m. _____at noon_____
5. 6:00 p.m. _____in the evening_____
6. 12:00 a.m. _____at midnight_____

Check your answers. See page 137.

LESSON E Writing

1 Read. Complete the sentences.

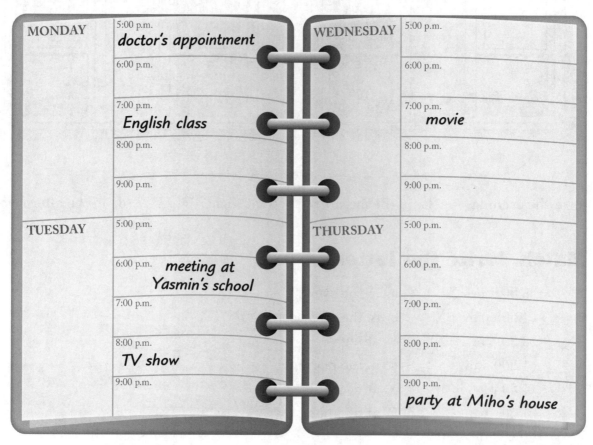

1. **A** What time is the
   _____ *party* _____?

   B At 9:00 on Thursday.

2. **A** What time is the doctor's
   _____ appointment _____?

   B At 5:00 on Monday.

3. **A** What time is the
   _____ TV show _____?

   B At 8:00 on Tuesday.

4. **A** What time is the English
   _____ class _____?

   B At 7:00 on Monday.

5. **A** What time is the
   _____ movie _____?

   B At 7:00 on Wednesday.

6. **A** What time is the
   _____ meeting at Yasmin's? school

   B At 6:00 on Tuesday.

Check your answers. See page 137.

2 Read. Complete the story.

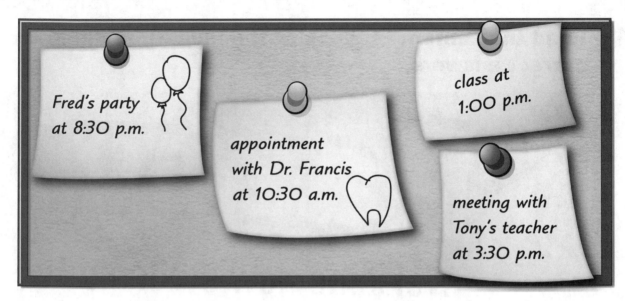

Jill is very busy today. Her ___*appointment*___ with

Dr. Francis is at 10:30. Her ___*class*___ is at 1:00.

Her meeting with Tony's teacher is at ___3:30 m___ in the

afternoon. Fred's party is at ___8:30___ in the evening.

3 Complete the memo. Use the story in Exercise 2.

memo

Time:	Event:
10:30	appointment
1:00 pm	class
3:30 pm	meeting with Tony's teacher
8:30 pm	party

1 **Read the sentences. Look at the invitation. Fill in the correct answers.**

1. It's a party for _____.
   ● students and teachers
   Ⓑ George Washington
   Ⓒ Alfonso Carillo

2. The party is on _____.
   Ⓐ Friday
   Ⓑ Saturday
   Ⓒ Sunday

3. The party is at _____.
   Ⓐ 8:00 a.m.
   Ⓑ 3:00 p.m.
   Ⓒ 8:00 p.m.

4. The party is _____.
   Ⓐ in the morning
   Ⓑ in the afternoon
   Ⓒ in the evening

Check your answers. See page 137.

2 **Use the code. Write the words.**

Code						
1=a	5=e	9=i	13=m	17=q	21=u	25=y
2=b	6=f	10=j	14=n	18=r	22=v	26=z
3=c	7=g	11=k	15=o	19=s	23=w	
4=d	8=h	12=l	16=p	20=t	24=x	

1. 16 1 18 20 25

   _p_ _a_ _r_ _t_ _y_

2. 3 12 1 19 19

   _c_ _l_ _a_ _s_ _s_

3. 5 22 5 14 9 14 7

   _e_ _v_ _e_ _n_ _i_ _n_ _g_

4. 13 15 18 14 9 14 7

   _m_ _o_ _r_ _n_ _i_ _n_ _g_

5. 13 9 4 14 9 7 8 20

   _m_ _i_ _d_ _n_ _i_ _g_ _h_ _t_

3 **Find the words from Exercise 2.**

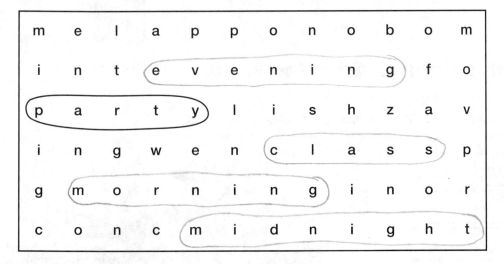

LESSON **A** Listening

1 **Look at the pictures. Match.**

1.

4.

a dress

2.

pants

5.

a shirt

shoes

socks

3.

6.

a T-shirt

2 **Look at the picture. Write the words.**

| a dress | pants | a shirt | shoes | socks | a T-shirt |

1. _____ *a shirt* _____

2. _____

3. _____

4. _____

5. _____

6. _____

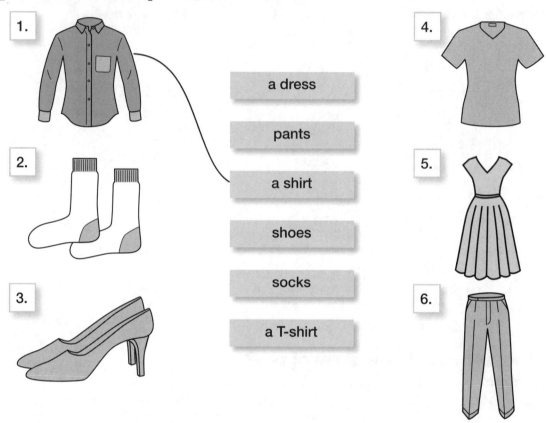

1.

2.

3.

4.

5.

6.

Check your answers. See page 137.

3 Listen and write.

TRACK 23

dress	pants	shirt	shoes	socks	T-shirt

1. The ___shoes___ are $39.00.
2. The ________ is $45.00.
3. The ________ are $10.99.
4. The ________ is $25.50.
5. The ________ is $40.99.
6. The ________ are $59.00.

4 Complete the puzzle. Use the words from Exercise 3.

Down ↓

1.

2.

3.

4.

Across →

5.

6.

Check your answers. See page 137.

LESSON B Clothing

Complete the words.

blouse	jacket	raincoat	skirt	sweater	tie

1. a __t__ i e
2. a s w ___ ___ t e r
3. a s k ___ ___ t

4. a j a c k ___ ___
5. a r ___ ___ n c o a t
6. a b l ___ ___ s e

2 **Complete the sentences. Use the words from Exercise 1.**

1. The _____raincoat_____ is $49.95.
2. The _____ is $24.95.
3. The _____ is $59.95.

4. The _____ is $19.99.
5. The _____ is $19.95.
6. The _____ is $32.00.

Check your answers. See page 137.

3 **Read. Write the words and the prices.**

Clothing for your family...

$42.50 $39.50 $29.99

ON SALE NOW!

$25.99 $24.50 $65.00

1. The tie is _____ *$25.99* _____ .

2. The _____ is $39.50.

3. The sweater is _____ .

4. The _____ is $29.99.

5. The skirt is _____ .

6. The _____ is $65.00.

Check your answers. See page 137.

LESSON C How much are the shoes?

1 Read the questions. Circle the correct answers.

1. How much are the ____?
   a. socks
   b. blouse
   c. tie

2. How much is the ____?
   a. shoes
   b. skirt
   c. socks

3. How much are the ____?
   a. tie
   b. skirt
   c. pants

4. How much is the ____?
   a. raincoat
   b. socks
   c. shoes

5. How much are the ____?
   a. tie
   b. sweater
   c. shoes

6. How much is the ____?
   a. shoes
   b. T-shirt
   c. pants

2 Write *is* or *are*.

1. **A** How much _____is_____ the tie?

   B $25.00.

2. **A** How much _____ the socks?

   B $1.99.

3. **A** How much _____ the blouse?

   B $29.99.

4. **A** How much _____ the pants?

   B $19.99.

5. **A** How much _____ the shoes?

   B $39.90.

6. **A** How much _____ the sweater?

   B $34.95.

Check your answers. See page 137.

3 Look at the picture. Write *is* or *are* and the prices.

1. **A** How much _____is_____ the blouse?

   B ___$42.00___.

2. **A** How much _____ the pants?

   B _____.

3. **A** How much _____ the socks?

   B _____.

4. **A** How much _____ the shirt?

   B _____.

5. **A** How much _____ the sweater?

   B _____.

6. **A** How much _____ the skirt?

   B _____.

Check your answers. See page 137.

LESSON D Reading

1 Read and circle the answers. Then listen.

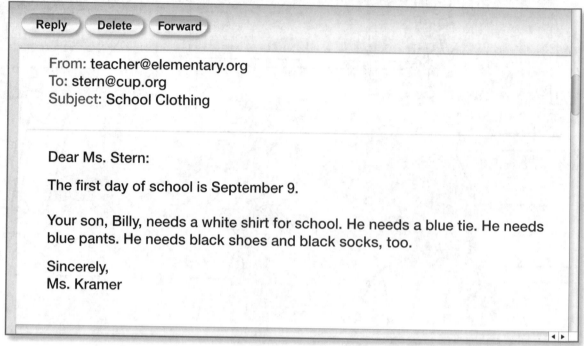

Reply   Delete   Forward

From: teacher@elementary.org
To: stern@cup.org
Subject: School Clothing

Dear Ms. Stern:

The first day of school is September 9.

Your son, Billy, needs a white shirt for school. He needs a blue tie. He needs blue pants. He needs black shoes and black socks, too.

Sincerely,
Ms. Kramer

1. Billy needs brown shoes.	Yes	(No)
2. Billy needs black socks.	Yes	No
3. Billy needs a blue tie.	Yes	No
4. Billy needs blue pants.	Yes	No
5. Billy needs a blue shirt.	Yes	No

2 What color is the clothing in Exercise 1? Write the words.

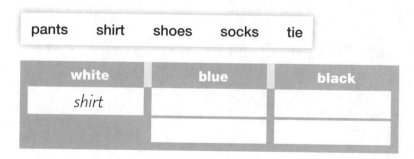

pants   shirt   shoes   socks   tie

white	blue	black
shirt		

Check your answers. See page 138.

3 **Look at the chart. Write the answers.**

Name	red	yellow	green	black	white	brown	blue
Sharmin			blouse	skirt			
Walter			tie	pants	shirt		
Lan		dress		shoes			
Omar	jacket					pants	sweater
Dora					blouse	shoes	skirt
Antonio	T-shirt	raincoat			socks		

1. **A** What color are Walter's pants?

   B _____Black_____.

2. **A** What color is Lan's dress?

   B _____.

3. **A** What color is Antonio's T-shirt?

   B _____.

4. **A** What color is Dora's blouse?

   B _____.

5. **A** What color is Sharmin's skirt?

   B _____.

6. **A** What color are Dora's shoes?

   B _____.

7. **A** What color is Omar's sweater?

   B _____.

8. **A** What color is Walter's tie?

   B _____.

LESSON E Writing

1 Complete the words.

1. <u>b</u> <u>l</u> o u s e

2. r a i n c ___ ___ t

3. j a ___ ___ e t

4. t i ___

5. s w e a t ___ ___

6. s k ___ r t

2 Look at the pictures. Write the words.

1. a _____blouse_____

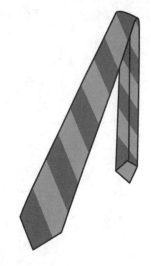

2. a _____

3. a _____

4. a _____

5. a _____

6. a _____

Check your answers. See page 138.

3 Complete the chart.

| blouse | jacket | raincoat | skirt | sweater |
| dress | pants | shoes | socks | tie |

Men's clothes	Men's and women's clothes	Women's clothes
	jacket	

4 Read. Complete the shopping list. Then listen.

TRACK 25

Francesca is shopping today with her family. They need new clothes.

Her mother Carmela needs a dress. Her husband Mario needs a shirt. Her son Jerome needs pants. Her daughter Lisa needs a raincoat. Francesca needs new shoes.

Francesca's Shopping List

Name	Clothing
Francesca	shoes
Lisa	
Jerome	
Carmela	
Mario	

Check your answers. See page 138.

1 **Look at the picture. Complete the receipt.**

Sales Receipt

The House of Clothes

32 Park Street
New York, NY 10013
(212) 555-7736

Clothing

_____tie_____ $18.00

_____ $30.00

_____ $35.00

_____ $40.00

Total: . . . . _____

Check your answers. See page 138.

2 Find the words.

black	brown	orange	purple	yellow
blue	green	pink	red	white

s	w	e	s	h	o	j	a	c	r
p	r	i	n	g	r	e	e	n	d
t	e	c	y	e	l	l	o	w	g
k	a	t	h	r	e	d	l	n	o
b	l	a	c	k	m	b	l	u	e
c	o	l	s	c	h	o	b	l	u
s	h	a	w	h	i	t	e	r	o
a	i	n	c	t	s	h	i	b	l
n	m	p	b	r	o	w	n	e	c
r	o	r	a	n	g	e	s	o	c
p	i	n	k	d	r	e	p	a	s
o	u	s	e	p	u	r	p	l	e

3 What is different? Cross it out.

1.	shirt	blouse	~~pants~~
2.	jacket	shoes	raincoat
3.	shoes	T-shirt	socks
4.	skirt	dress	pants
5.	blouse	tie	dress

Check your answers. See page 138.

LESSON A Listening

1 Complete the words.

1. m e c h a n _i_ _c_

2. s e r v ___ ___

3. s a l e s p e r ___ ___ ___

4. r e c e p t i o n ___ ___ ___

5. c u s t o d ___ ___ ___

6. c a s h ___ ___ ___

2 Find the words from Exercise 1.

t	r	c	a	m	n	i	v	z	q	u	i
s	a	l	e	s	p	e	r	s	o	n	t
e	c	t	r	o	k	j	u	m	g	l	u
p	t	o	s	e	r	v	e	r	t	u	h
c	a	s	h	i	e	r	e	n	o	s	l
l	i	e	s	t	w	a	p	s	h	e	a
r	e	c	e	p	t	i	o	n	i	s	t
r	o	n	p	e	c	i	k	m	a	r	r
c	c	u	s	t	o	d	i	a	n	t	e
i	e	u	z	t	i	o	n	w	a	i	z
k	m	e	c	h	a	n	i	c	g	o	s

Check your answers. See page 138.

3 Listen and number.

TRACK 26

Fatima

Edward

Gabriel

Cecilia

Bruno

Cathy

4 Look at the pictures in Exercise 3. Match.

1. Fatima   mechanic
2. Cecilia   cashier
3. Bruno   receptionist
4. Gabriel   custodian
5. Cathy   server
6. Edward   salesperson

Check your answers. See page 138.

LESSON **B** Job duties

1 Check (✓) the job duties.

Jobs	Sells clothes	Cleans buildings	Serves food	Answers the phone	Counts money	Fixes cars
server			✓			
mechanic						
salesperson						
receptionist						
custodian						
cashier						

2 Write the job duties.

answers the phone   counts money   sells clothes
cleans buildings   fixes cars   serves food

1. A server _____ *serves food* _____.

2. A receptionist _____.

3. A cashier _____.

4. A salesperson _____.

5. A custodian _____.

6. A mechanic _____.

3 Write the job duties.

1. _____ *fixes cars* _____

2. _____

3. _____

Check your answers. See pages 138–139.

4 **Look at the pictures. Write the correct answers. Then listen.**

TRACK 27

1. **A** What does she do?

   B She _____*sells clothes*_____.

2. **A** What does he do?

   B He _____.

3. **A** What does she do?

   B She _____.

4. **A** What does he do?

   B He _____.

5. **A** What does she do?

   B She _____.

6. **A** What does he do?

   B He _____.

Check your answers. See page 139.

LESSON C Does he sell clothes?

Study the chart on page 127.

1 Look at the pictures. Circle the correct answers.

1. Does he fix cars?
   a. Yes, he does.
   b. No, he doesn't.

2. Does she answer the phone?
   a. Yes, she does.
   b. No, she doesn't.

3. Does he clean buildings?
   a. Yes, he does.
   b. No, he doesn't.

4. Does she count money?
   a. Yes, she does.
   b. No, she doesn't.

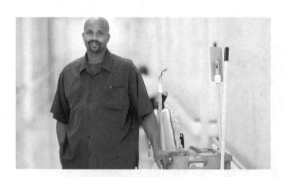

5. Does he serve food?
   a. Yes, he does.
   b. No, he doesn't.

6. Does she sell clothes?
   a. Yes, she does.
   b. No, she doesn't.

Check your answers. See page 139.

2 **Look at the picture. Complete the sentences.**

1. **A** _____Does_____ Naoko _____serve_____ food?

   B Yes, she _____does_____.

2. **A** _____ Juan _____ money?

   B Yes, he _____.

3. **A** _____ Imelda _____ the phone?

   B No, she _____.

4. **A** _____ Franco _____ buildings?

   B Yes, he _____.

5. **A** _____ Soo Yeun _____ cars?

   B No, she _____.

6. **A** _____ Kevin _____ clothes?

   B Yes, he _____.

Check your answers. See page 139.

LESSON D Reading

TRACK 28

1 **Read and complete the sentences. Then listen.**

Dear Mom,

   I have good news! The children have jobs for the summer. In the morning, Nicolas is a mechanic. He fixes cars. In the evening, he is a server. He serves food. Lydia is a teacher's aide in the morning. She helps the teacher. In the evening, she is a salesperson. She sells clothes. In the afternoon, I am a receptionist. I answer the phone. Our whole family is very busy!

   How are you? I miss you.

                                      Love,
                                      Tanya

1. **A** What does Lydia do in the evening?

   B She _sells clothes_ .
   She is a _salesperson_ .

2. **A** What does Nicolas do in the morning?

   B He _____ .
   He is a _____ .

3. **A** What does Lydia do in the morning?

   B She _____ .
   She is a _____ .

4. **A** What does Nicolas do in the evening?

   B He _____ .
   He is a _____ .

5. **A** What does Tanya do in the afternoon?

   B She _____ .
   She is a _____ .

Check your answers. See page 139.

2 Look at the pictures. Complete the sentences.

bus driver	painter	teacher's aide
homemaker	plumber	truck driver

1. **A** What does he do?

   B He's a _____truck driver_____.

2. **A** What does she do?

   B She's a _____.

3. **A** What does he do?

   B He's a _____.

4. **A** What does she do?

   B She's a _____.

5. **A** What does he do?

   B He's a _____.

6. **A** What does she do?

   B She's a _____.

Check your answers. See page 139.

LESSON E Writing

1 Complete the words.

1. s e l l s __c__ __l__ o t h e s   4. f i x ___ ___ c a r s

2. c ___ ___ n t s m o n e y   5. ___ ___ e a n s b u i l d i n g s

3. ___ e r v e ___ f o o d   6. ___ ___ i v e s a b u s

2 Write the words.

| buildings | bus | cars | clothes | food | money | phone |

1. salesperson: sells _____*clothes*_____

2. server: serves _____

3. custodian: cleans _____

4. cashier: counts _____

5. mechanic: fixes _____

6. bus driver: drives a _____

7. receptionist: answers the _____

3 Look at the pictures. Complete the sentences.

1. She is a _____.   2. He is a _____.   3. She is a _____.
   She cleans __*buildings*__.   He counts _____.   She drives a _____.

Check your answers. See page 139.

4 Look at the pictures. Complete the letter.

Dear Aunt Rose,

How are you? We are all busy and happy. We have new jobs! Levon is a

_____server_____ at a restaurant on
1

State Street. He _____
2

food. Tamar is a _____.
3

She _____ a bus.
4

I am a _____. I
5

_____ clothes.
6

Write soon.

Love,

Rita

5 Complete the sentences. Use information from Exercise 4.

1. _____ sells clothes.

2. _____ is a bus driver.

3. _____ works at a restaurant.

LESSON F Another view

1 Read the sentences. Look at the ads. Then fill in the correct answers.

HELP WANTED

JOB 1
Server
$8.00 an hour
6:00 a.m. – 11:00 a.m.
Call 555-2192

JOB 2
Receptionist
$12.00 an hour
Monday – Friday
Call 555-8743

JOB 3
Truck Driver
$10.00 an hour
Part-time work
Call 555-3370

JOB 4
Plumber
$18.00 an hour
Work evenings
E-mail:
plumbers46@cup.com

1. Job 1 is for a ____ .
   ● server
   Ⓑ plumber
   Ⓒ receptionist

2. Job 2 is for a ____ .
   Ⓐ plumber
   Ⓑ truck driver
   Ⓒ receptionist

3. For Job 3, call ____ .
   Ⓐ 555-8743
   Ⓑ 555-3370
   Ⓒ 555-2192

4. For Job 2, call ____ .
   Ⓐ 555-8743
   Ⓑ 555-3370
   Ⓒ 555-2192

5. Job 4 is ____ .
   Ⓐ in the morning
   Ⓑ in the evening
   Ⓒ at night

6. Job 1 is ____ .
   Ⓐ in the morning
   Ⓑ in the evening
   Ⓒ at night

Check your answers. See page 139.

2 Write the words.

bus driver	cashier	mechanic	painter	plumber	server

_m_ _e_ _c_ h _a_ _n_ _i_ _c_

o

m

___ e ___ ___ ___ ___

___ l ___ m ___ ___ ___

___ a ___ ___ ___ ___

k

___ ___ ___ ___ ___ e ___

___ ___ ___ ___ r ___ ___ ___

3 Look at the chart. Complete the sentences.

	drive a bus	count money	fix cars	drive a truck
Ted	✓			
Jessica				✓
Rashid			✓	
Irene		✓		

1. **A** What's Ted's job?

   B He is a ___bus driver___.

   A What does he do?

   B He ___drives a bus___.

2. **A** What's Irene's job?

   B She is a _____.

   A What does she do?

   B She _____.

3. **A** What's Rashid's job?

   B He is a _____.

   A What does he do?

   B He _____.

4. **A** What's Jessica's job?

   B She is a _____.

   A What does she do?

   B She _____.

Check your answers. See page 139.

LESSON **A** Listening

1 **Write the words.**

| bed | dishes | homework | laundry | dishes | lunch |

1. washing the   _d_ _i_ _s_ _h_ _e_ _s_
2. doing ____ ____ ____ ____ ____ ____ ____ ____
3. making ____ ____ ____ ____ ____
4. doing the ____ ____ ____ ____ ____ ____ ____
5. making the ____ ____ ____
6. drying the ____ ____ ____ ____ ____ ____

2 **Look at the pictures. Write the words.**

1. ___*making lunch*___   2. _____   3. _____

3 **Circle the words. Then write.**

1. _____*washing*_____ the dishes
   (washing) making

2. _____ lunch
   making   drying

3. _____ homework
   doing   washing

4. _____ the dishes
   drying   making

5. _____ the bed
   making   drying

6. _____ the laundry
   making   doing

Check your answers. See page 139.

4 Listen and number.

TRACK 29

5 Look at the picture in Exercise 4. Write the words.

doing homework	drying the dishes	making the bed
doing the laundry	making lunch	washing the dishes

1. _____*drying the dishes*_____

2. _____

3. _____

4. _____

5. _____

6. _____

Check your answers. See page 139.

LESSON B Outside chores

1 **Unscramble the letters.**

1. n t c g i u t   _____ the grass

2. t n t i g e g   _____ the mail

3. k g n i a t   t u o   _____ the trash

4. k w g l a n i   _____ the dog

5. r i n g t a w e   _____ the grass

6. h s w a g n i   _____ the car

2 **Look at the picture. Circle the chores.**

1. taking out the trash   (cutting the grass)

2. cutting the grass   taking out the trash

3. getting the mail   walking the dog

4. walking the dog   cutting the grass

5. watering the grass   walking the dog

6. getting the mail   washing the car

Check your answers. See page 140.

3 Look at the pictures. Write the words.

Cutting   Getting   Taking out   Walking   Washing   Watering

1. **A** What is she doing?

   B ___*Watering*___ the grass.

2. **A** What is he doing?

   B _____ the grass.

3. **A** What is she doing?

   B _____ the mail.

4. **A** What is he doing?

   B _____ the car.

5. **A** What is she doing?

   B _____ the trash.

6. **A** What is he doing?

   B _____ the dog.

Check your answers. See page 140.

LESSON C What are they doing?

Study the chart on page 127.

1 Match.

1. drying   the bed
2. making   the trash
3. getting   the laundry
4. taking out   the dishes
5. washing   the dog
6. doing   the grass
7. cutting   the car
8. walking   the mail

2 Circle the correct answers. Write. Then listen.

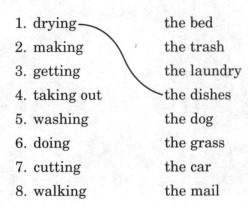

TRACK 30

1. **A** What _____*are*_____ they doing?
           is   (are)

   B Getting the _____*mail*_____.
           trash   (mail)

2. **A** What _____ he doing?
           is   are

   B Making _____.
           dinner   laundry

3. **A** What _____ she doing?
           is   are

   B Cutting the _____.
           dishes   grass

4. **A** What _____ they doing?
           is   are

   B Drying the _____.
           trash   dishes

5. **A** What _____ he doing?
           is   are

   B Walking the _____.
           dog   laundry

6. **A** What _____ she doing?
           is   are

   B Taking out the _____.
           trash   grass

Check your answers. See page 140.

3 Look at the pictures. Complete the sentences.

1. **A** What _____is_____ she doing?

   B _Making_ the bed.

2. **A** What _____ they doing?

   B _____ lunch.

3. **A** What _____ she doing?

   B _____ the mail.

4. **A** What _____ they doing?

   B _____ the grass.

5. **A** What _____ she doing?

   B _____ the dishes.

6. **A** What _____ he doing?

   B _____ out the trash.

Check your answers. See page 140.

LESSON **D** Reading

TRACK 31

> The Gomez family is busy this morning.
> Bonita is washing the dishes in the kitchen.
> Magda is doing homework in the living room.
> Outside, Ramon is cutting the grass. Manuel
> and Leon are washing the car. Luisa is taking
> out the trash.

1. Bonita is doing homework.   Yes (No)

2. Luisa is taking out the trash.   Yes   No

3. Magda is washing the dishes.   Yes   No

4. Manuel and Leon are washing the car.   Yes   No

5. Ramon is cutting the grass.   Yes   No

2 **Complete the sentences.**

1. What are Manuel and Leon doing?

   They are _____*washing the car*_____.

2. What is Bonita doing?

   She is _____.

3. What is Ramon doing?

   He is _____.

4. What is Magda doing?

   She is _____.

5. What is Luisa doing?

   She is _____.

3 Look at the pictures. Write the words.

bathroom	dining room	laundry room
bedroom	kitchen	living room

1. ___bathroom___

2. _____

3. _____

4. _____

5. _____

6. _____

4 Circle the correct rooms for the chores.

	Chores	Room	
1.	drying the dishes	laundry room	(kitchen)
2.	making the bed	bedroom	bathroom
3.	washing the dishes	kitchen	bedroom
4.	doing the laundry	living room	laundry room
5.	making lunch	kitchen	bathroom

Check your answers. See page 140.

LESSON E Writing

1 Complete the words.

1. d _r_ _y_ _i_ _n_ _g_ the dishes
2. w ___ ___ ___ ___ ___ ___ the dishes
3. m ___ ___ ___ ___ ___ lunch
4. d ___ ___ ___ ___ homework
5. m ___ ___ ___ ___ ___ the bed
6. d ___ ___ ___ ___ the laundry

2 Look at the chart. Write the chores.

Chore	Sun	Min	Dae	Chul	Soo	Chin
do homework	✓					
make the bed			✓			
make lunch				✓		
wash the dishes						✓
dry the dishes					✓	
do the laundry		✓				

1. Sun is _____ _doing homework_ _____.
2. Dae is _____.
3. Soo is _____.
4. Chin is _____.
5. Min is _____.
6. Chul is _____.

Check your answers. See page 140.

3 Look at the picture. Complete the chore chart.

Name	Chore
Justin	*doing the laundry*
Melissa	
Henry	
Penny	
Bill	
Erica	

Check your answers. See page 140.

LESSON F Another view

1 **Read the sentences. Look at the calendar. Fill in the correct answers.**

Monday	Tuesday	Wednesday	Thursday	Friday
Erin	Adam	Andy	Suzy	Sara
beds	grass	car	laundry	trash

1. Today is Wednesday. Andy is _____.
   Ⓐ making the beds
   ● washing the car
   Ⓒ cutting the grass

2. Today is Monday. Erin is _____.
   Ⓐ making the beds
   Ⓑ taking out the trash
   Ⓒ doing the laundry

3. Today is Thursday. Suzy is _____.
   Ⓐ cutting the grass
   Ⓑ making the beds
   Ⓒ doing the laundry

4. Today is Tuesday. Adam is _____.
   Ⓐ cutting the grass
   Ⓑ washing the car
   Ⓒ taking out the trash

5. Today is Friday. Sara is _____.
   Ⓐ making the beds
   Ⓑ doing the laundry
   Ⓒ taking out the trash

2 **Look at the calendar in Exercise 1. Complete the sentences.**

1. It's Wednesday. Andy _____ the car.

2. It's Monday. Erin _____ the beds.

3. It's Friday. Sara _____ the trash.

4. It's Tuesday. Adam _____ the grass.

5. It's Thursday. Suzy _____ the laundry.

Check your answers. See page 140.

3 Unscramble the letters. Write the words.

bathroom	dining room	laundry room
bedroom	kitchen	living room

1. b t h a o o r m   _____ *bathroom* _____

2. r o m o b d e   _____

3. k c h n e t i   _____

4. n d i g n i o r o m   _____

5. v i n g l i m o r o   _____

6. y r d u n l a m r o o   _____

4 Write the rooms.

1. making lunch   _____ *kitchen* _____

2. doing the laundry   _____

3. drying the dishes   _____

4. making the bed   _____

5. washing the dishes   _____

5 Complete the chart.

cutting the grass	making the bed	washing the dishes
drying the dishes	walking the dog	watering the grass
making lunch	washing the car	

Chores inside the house	Chores outside the house
drying the dishes	*cutting the grass*

Check your answers. See page 140.

LESSON A Listening

1 Complete the words.

1. f _i_ s h
2. s w ___ m
3. d ___ n c e
4. e x ___ ___ c i s e
5. p l a y c ___ ___ d s
6. p l ___ ___ b a s k ___ ___ b a l l

2 Find the words.

| basketball | cards | dance | exercise | fish | play | swim |

b	i	c	y	t	a	b	l	s	h
p	d	a	n	c	e	y	z	f	i
e	x	e	r	p	l	a	y	m	b
e	x	e	r	c	i	s	e	d	o
c	a	r	d	s	m	o	n	w	t
e	y	f	i	s	w	i	m	y	a
d	a	v	n	g	e	l	u	s	w
n	c	f	i	s	h	i	m	b	a
b	a	s	k	e	t	b	a	l	l
d	s	z	o	n	f	r	e	x	p

Check your answers. See page 141.

3 **Listen and number. Then write.**

TRACK 32

| exercise | fish | play basketball | play cards | swim |

1. _____ *swim* _____

2. _____

3. _____

4. _____

5. _____

Check your answers. See page 141.

LESSON **B** Around the house

1 **Match. Then write the words.**

1. read ——— in the garden

2. play TV

3. listen to the guitar

4. watch magazines

5. work music

read magazines

_____

_____

_____

_____

2 **Look at the pictures. Write the words.**

1. **A** What does she like to do?

   B Listen to _____ _music_ _____.

2. **A** What does he like to do?

   B Watch _____.

3. **A** What does she like to do?

   B Play _____.

4. **A** What does he like to do?

   B Work _____.

5. **A** What does she like to do?

   B Read _____.

Check your answers. See page 141.

3 **Look at the picture. Write the words.**

Cook	Play the guitar	Watch TV
Listen to music	Read magazines	Work in the garden

1. What does Sarita like to do? _____ *Cook* _____.

2. What does Steve like to do? _____.

3. What does Lola like to do? _____.

4. What does Marco like to do? _____.

5. What does Kaitlin like to do? _____.

6. What does Dennis like to do? _____.

Check your answers. See page 141.

LESSON C I like to watch TV.

Study the chart on pages 127–128.

1 **Write *like* or *likes*. Then listen.**

TRACK 33

1. **A** What does she like to do?

   B She _____*likes*_____ to work in the garden.

2. **A** What does he like to do?

   B He _____ to play the guitar.

3. **A** What do they like to do?

   B They _____ to watch TV.

4. **A** What does she like to do?

   B She _____ to read magazines.

5. **A** What do they like to do?

   B They _____ to play cards.

6. **A** What do you like to do?

   B I _____ to cook.

7. **A** What does she like to do?

   B She _____ to play basketball.

8. **A** What do you like to do?

   B I _____ to play soccer.

Check your answers. See page 141.

2 Look at the pictures. Circle *like* or *likes*. Complete the sentences.

1. **A** What does he like to do?

   B He ___*likes*___ to ___*exercise*___.
   like (likes)

2. **A** What does she like to do?

   B She _____ to _____.
   like   likes

3. **A** What does she like to do?

   B She _____ to _____.
   like   likes

4. **A** What does he like to do?

   B He _____ to _____.
   like   likes

5. **A** What do they like to do?

   B They _____ to _____.
   like   likes

6. **A** What do they like to do?

   B They _____ to _____.
   like   likes

Check your answers. See page 141.

LESSON **D** Reading

1 **Read and circle the answers. Then listen.**

TRACK 34

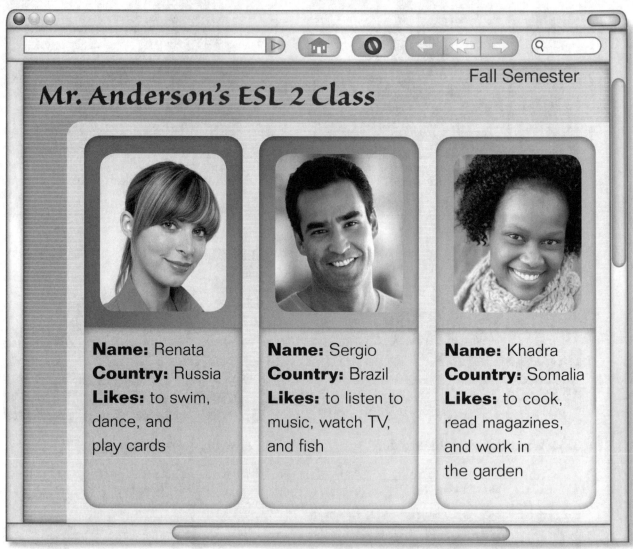

Fall Semester

Mr. Anderson's ESL 2 Class

Name: Renata
Country: Russia
Likes: to swim, dance, and play cards

Name: Sergio
Country: Brazil
Likes: to listen to music, watch TV, and fish

Name: Khadra
Country: Somalia
Likes: to cook, read magazines, and work in the garden

1. Renata likes to swim.   (Yes)   No

2. Sergio likes to cook.   Yes   No

3. Khadra likes to play cards.   Yes   No

4. Renata likes to work in the garden.   Yes   No

5. Sergio likes to watch TV.   Yes   No

6. Khadra likes to read magazines.   Yes   No

Check your answers. See page 141.

2 What do they like to do? Look and match.

1.

2.

3.

4.

5.

travel

shop

volunteer

exercise

go to the movies

Check your answers. See page 141.

LESSON E Writing

1 Complete the words.

| cook | dance | fish | shop | swim | volunteer |

1. _s_ _w_ _i_ m

2. ___ ___ ___ h

3. ___ ___ ___ k

4. ___ ___ ___ p

5. ___ ___ ___ ___ e

6. ___ ___ ___ ___ ___ ___ ___ r

2 Read. Complete the sentences.

	work in the garden	fish	volunteer	play cards	swim
Flor	✓				
Alvaro				✓	
Vera					✓
Brian		✓			
Kim			✓		

1. Flor likes to ____work in the garden____.

2. Vera likes to _____.

3. Kim likes to _____.

4. Brian likes to _____.

5. Alvaro likes to _____.

Check your answers. See page 141.

3 **Complete the sentences.**

| exercise | go | listen to | play | read | visit | watch |

1. Jason likes to _____*play*_____ basketball on Saturday.

2. Jason likes to _____ TV on Thursday.

3. Jason likes to _____ magazines on Wednesday.

4. Jason likes to _____ to the movies on Sunday.

5. Jason likes to _____ friends on Friday.

6. Jason likes to _____ on Monday.

7. Jason likes to _____ music on Tuesday.

4 **Write the information from Exercise 3 on the calendar.**

Jason's Calendar

Sunday	Monday	Tuesday	Wednesday	Thursday	Friday	Saturday
1	2	3	4	5	6	7
						play basketball

Check your answers. See page 141.

LESSON F Another view

1 **Read the sentences. Look at the catalog.**
Fill in the correct answers.

Community Center Classes
September 2 to December 12

Learn to dance!
Monday and Wednesday
11:00 a.m. – 12:30 p.m.
Room 110
$95.00

Learn to swim!
Tuesday and Thursday
9:00 a.m. – 10:30 a.m.
Pool
$100.00

Learn to play basketball!
Friday
2:30 p.m. – 4:30 p.m.
Room 115
$75.00

Learn to cook!
Monday and Wednesday
10:30 a.m. – 12:00 p.m.
Room 121
$85.00

1. The dance class is in Room _____.
   ● 110
   Ⓑ 115
   Ⓒ 121

2. The cooking class is in Room _____.
   Ⓐ 110
   Ⓑ 115
   Ⓒ 121

3. The basketball class is _____.
   Ⓐ in the morning
   Ⓑ in the afternoon
   Ⓒ in the evening

4. The swimming class is _____.
   Ⓐ in the morning
   Ⓑ in the afternoon
   Ⓒ in the evening

5. The dance class is _____.
   Ⓐ $85.00
   Ⓑ $95.00
   Ⓒ $100.00

6. The basketball class is _____.
   Ⓐ $75.00
   Ⓑ $85.00
   Ⓒ $100.00

Check your answers. See page 141.

2 Unscramble the letters. Write the words.

listen to music	play cards	read magazines
play basketball	play the guitar	visit friends

1. y a p l   d s a r c _____ *play cards* _____
2. s i t v i   f i r n e s d _____
3. a y l p   e h t   t r a i u g _____
4. a e d r   g z a m n i e a s _____
5. l y a p   k b l s e t a a l b _____
6. n e t s l i   o t   c s i u m _____

3 Complete the chart.

go to the movies	run	shop	travel	visit friends	volunteer

Costs money $$$	Costs no money ~~$$$~~
travel	

4 Complete the chart.

dance	play basketball	read magazines	watch TV
go online	play cards	run	
listen to music	play soccer	swim	

Exercise	No exercise
dance	

Reference

Possessive adjectives

Questions

	my	
	your	
	his	
	her	
What's	its	phone number?
	our	
	your	
	their	

Answers

Your	
My	
His	
Her	phone number is 555-3348.
Its	
Your	
Our	
Their	

Present of *be*

Yes / No questions

Am	I	
Are	you	
Is	he	
Is	she	
Is	it	from Somalia?
Are	we	
Are	you	
Are	they	

Short answers

	you	are.
	I	am.
	he	is.
	she	is.
Yes,	it	is.
	you	are.
	we	are.
	they	are.

	you aren't.
	I'm not.
	he isn't.
	she isn't.
No,	it isn't.
	you aren't.
	we aren't.
	they aren't.

aren't	=	are not
isn't	=	is not

Contractions

I'm	=	I am
You're	=	You are
He's	=	He is
She's	=	She is
It's	=	It is
We're	=	We are
You're	=	You are
They're	=	They are

Simple present

Yes / No questions

Do	I	
Do	you	
Does	he	
Does	she	
Does	it	sell clothes?
Do	we	
Do	you	
Do	they	

Short answers

	you	do.
	I	do.
	he	does.
Yes,	she	does.
	it	does.
	you	do.
	we	do.
	they	do.

	you	don't.
	I	don't.
	he	doesn't.
	she	doesn't.
No,	it	doesn't.
	you	don't.
	we	don't.
	they	don't.

don't	=	do not
doesn't	=	does not

Present continuous

Questions with *What*

	am	I	
	are	you	
	is	he	
What	is	she	doing?
	is	it	
	are	we	
	are	you	
	are	they	

Short answers

Working.

Simple present of *like to* + verb

Questions with *What*

	do	I	
	do	you	
	does	he	
What	does	she	like to do?
	does	it	
	do	we	
	do	you	
	do	they	

Answers

You	like	
I	like	
He	likes	
She	likes	
It	likes	to swim.
You	like	
We	like	
They	like	

Yes / No questions

Do	I	
Do	you	
Does	he	
Does	she	like to swim?
Does	it	
Do	we	
Do	you	
Do	they	

Short answers

	you	do.
	I	do.
	he	does.
Yes,	she	does.
	it	does.
	you	do.
	we	do.
	they	do.

	you	don't.
	I	don't.
	he	doesn't.
No,	she	doesn't.
	it	doesn't.
	you	don't.
	we	don't.
	they	don't.

Simple present of *have*

Yes / No questions

Do	I	
Do	you	
Does	he	
Does	she	have a sister?
Do	we	
Do	you	
Do	they	

Short answers

	you	do.
	I	do.
	he	does.
Yes,	she	does.
	you	do.
	we	do.
	they	do.

	you	don't.
	I	don't.
	he	doesn't.
No,	she	doesn't.
	you	don't.
	we	don't.
	they	don't.

Affirmative statements

I	have	
You	have	
He	has	
She	has	a sister.
We	have	
You	have	
They	have	

Negative statements

I	don't		
You	don't		
He	doesn't		
She	doesn't	have	a sister.
We	don't		
You	don't		
They	don't		

Capitalization rules

Begin the first word in a sentence with a capital letter.	**M**y name is Nancy. **W**here is Ivan from?
Begin the names of months and days of the week with a capital letter.	**J**anuary **S**unday
Begin the names of countries, cities, streets, and other places with a capital letter.	**M**exico　　**F**lorida　　**T**ampa **P**ine **A**venue　The **C**lothes **P**lace
Begin the names of people with a capital letter.	**S**ara **G**arza **E**rnesto **D**elgado
Begin family relationship words with a capital when they are part of a name. Do not begin family relationship words with a capital when they are not part of a name.	I like **U**ncle Eduardo. My **u**ncle is Eduardo.
Begin a title with a capital when it is part of the name.	**M**rs. Navarro **D**r. Martin

Cardinal numbers

0 zero	10 ten	20 twenty	30 thirty	40 forty
1 one	11 eleven	21 twenty-one	31 thirty-one	50 fifty
2 two	12 twelve	22 twenty-two	32 thirty-two	60 sixty
3 three	13 thirteen	23 twenty-three	33 thirty-three	70 seventy
4 four	14 fourteen	24 twenty-four	34 thirty-four	80 eighty
5 five	15 fifteen	25 twenty-five	35 thirty-five	90 ninety
6 six	16 sixteen	26 twenty-six	36 thirty-six	100 one hundred
7 seven	17 seventeen	27 twenty-seven	37 thirty-seven	1,000 one thousand
8 eight	18 eighteen	28 twenty-eight	38 thirty-eight	
9 nine	19 nineteen	29 twenty-nine	39 thirty-nine	

Ordinal numbers

1st first	11th eleventh	21st twenty-first	31st thirty-first
2nd second	12th twelfth	22nd twenty-second	
3rd third	13th thirteenth	23rd twenty-third	
4th fourth	14th fourteenth	24th twenty-fourth	
5th fifth	15th fifteenth	25th twenty-fifth	
6th sixth	16th sixteenth	26th twenty-sixth	
7th seventh	17th seventeenth	27th twenty-seventh	
8th eighth	18th eighteenth	28th twenty-eighth	
9th ninth	19th nineteenth	29th twenty-ninth	
10th tenth	20th twentieth	30th thirtieth	

Metric equivalents

1 inch = 25 millimeters	1 dry ounce = 28 grams	1 fluid ounce = 30 milliliters
1 foot = 30 centimeters	1 pound = .45 kilograms	1 quart = .95 liters
1 yard = .9 meters	1 mile = 1.6 kilometers	1 gallon = 3.8 liters

Converting Farenheit temperatures to Celsius

Subtract 30 and divide by 2.
Example: 80°F − 30 = 50; divided by 2 = 25
80°F = approximately 25°C

Answer key

Welcome

Exercise 1 page 2
D, H, L, P, T, X

Exercise 2 page 2
c, f, i, l, o, r, u, x

Exercise 3 page 3
a. 1   d. 3   g. 4
b. 6   e. 9   h. 7
c. 5   f. 8   i. 2

Exercise 4 page 4
1, 4, 7, 10, 13, 16, 19

Exercise 5 page 4
one, three, five, seven, nine, twelve, fourteen, sixteen, eighteen, twenty

Exercise 6 page 5
1. four   5. two
2. one   6. five
3. three   7. six
4. eight   8. seven

Unit 1: Personal information

Lesson A: Listening

Exercise 1 page 6
1. first name
2. last name
3. country
4. area code
5. phone number

Exercise 2 page 6
1. Anna
2. Lopez
3. Mexico
4. 254
5. 555-2992

Exercise 3 page 7
1. first name – Marta
2. last name – Zaya
3. phone number – 555-2763
4. area code – 619

Exercise 4 page 7
1. phone number
2. area code
3. last name
4. first name

Exercise 5 page 7
1. first name
2. last name
3. area code
4. phone number

Lesson B: Countries

Exercise 1 page 8
1. f   3. e   5. b   7. h
2. a   4. c   6. d   8. g

Exercise 2 page 8
1. China
2. Brazil
3. Russia
4. Mexico
5. Somalia
6. Haiti

Exercise 3 page 9
1. Somalia
2. The United States
3. China
4. Brazil
5. Russia
6. Mexico
7. Haiti
8. Vietnam

Lesson C: What's your name?

Exercise 1 page 10
1. her   5. her
2. his   6. his
3. his   7. her
4. her   8. his

Exercise 2 page 11
1. your   5. your
2. My   6. My
3. your   7. your
4. My   8. My

Exercise 3 page 11
Manuel
Alvez
917
555-9845

Lesson D: Reading

Exercise 1 page 12
1. Boris Egorov
2. Egorov
3. Boris
4. Russia

Exercise 2 page 12
1. c   2. a   3. d   4. b

Exercise 3 page 13
February, March, May, June, August, September, November

Exercise 4 page 13
1. In June
2. In January
3. In February
4. In April
5. In July

Lesson E: Writing

Exercise 1 page 14

1. country
2. area code
3. first name
4. phone number
5. last name

Exercise 2 page 14

1. first name
2. last name
3. area code
4. phone number
5. China

Exercise 3 page 15

1. Emma
2. Harris
3. 407
4. 555-6524

Exercise 4 page 15

First name: Octavio
Last name: Diaz
Birthday: December 7, 1995
Country: Mexico
Area code: 206
Phone number: 555-3687

Lesson F: Another view

Exercise 1 page 16

1. C   4. A
2. B   5. B
3. A   6. C

Exercise 2 page 17

1. c o (c o u n t r y) t e
2. m e (n a m e) a n
3. l j u l (J u n e) J y
4. m o n (m o n t h) t h
5. d a y (b i r t h d a y) b i
6. p h (p h o n e) p n

Exercise 3 page 17

1. August   5. Russia
2. 555-9832   6. January
3. 972   7. Brazil
4. Somalia

Exercise 4 page 17

1: January   12: December
4: April   3: March
8: August   2: February
7: July   10: October
5: May   9: September
11: November   6: June

Unit 2: At school

Lesson A: Listening

Exercise 1 page 18

1. a chair
2. a notebook
3. a desk
4. a book
5. a computer

Exercise 2 page 19

(L to R:) 3, 5, 4, 1, 2
1. desk
2. notebook
3. chair
4. pencil
5. book

Exercise 3 page 19

1. book   4. computer
2. notebook   5. pencil
3. desk   6. chair

Lesson B: Classroom objects

Exercise 1 page 20

1. stapler
2. ruler
3. dictionary
4. eraser
5. paper

Exercise 2 page 20

(d i c t i o n a r y)
p i n d (e r a s e r)
l a e (s t a p l e r)
(p a p e r) b v z p x
w s b a l o y (p e n)
q u y s f (r u l e r)

Exercise 3 page 21

1. dictionary 4. ruler
2. paper   5. stapler
3. pen   6. eraser

Exercise 4 page 21

1. pen   4. dictionary
2. stapler   5. ruler
3. eraser   6. paper

Lesson C: Where's my pencil?

Exercise 1 page 22

1. c   3. a   5. d
2. e   4. b

Exercise 2 page 22

1. In
2. On
3. Under
4. On
5. On

Exercise 3 page 23

1. On the desk
2. Under the notebook
3. In the desk
4. On the floor
5. On the desk
6. On the chair

Lesson D: Reading

Exercise 1 page 24

1. n o t (n o t e b o o k) t e
2. e r (e r a s e r) a s
3. c (c o m p u t e r) t e r
4. e n (p e n c i l) i l p
5. e s k (d e s k) d e n c i l
6. k o b o o o k (b o o k)

Exercise 2 page 24

1. You need a dictionary.
2. You need a pencil.
3. You need a notebook.
4. You need a ruler.
5. You need an eraser.

Exercise 3 page 25

1: Sunday
6: Friday
2: Monday
4: Wednesday
5: Thursday
3: Tuesday
7: Saturday

Exercise 4 page 25

```
            S u n d a y
M o n d a y
            t
            T u e s d a y
            F r i d a y
        We d n e s d a y
            a
T h u r s d a y
```

Exercise 5 page 25

1. Friday
2. Thursday
3. Tuesday

Lesson E: Writing

Exercise 1 page 26

1. notebook   4. eraser
2. dictionary   5. pencil
3. ruler   6. stapler

Exercise 2 page 27

1. on   4. in
2. on   5. under
3. on   6. in

Exercise 3 page 27

1. pencil   4. paper
2. eraser   5. dictionary
3. ruler   6. notebook

Exercise 4 page 27

1. pencil   4. paper
2. eraser   5. dictionary
3. ruler   6. notebook

Lesson F: Another view

Exercise 1 page 28

1. C   3. A   5. A
2. B   4. C   6. B

Exercise 2 page 29

Across
1. pen
4. dictionary
5. ruler
7. eraser
8. desk

Down
2. notebook
3. stapler
6. pencil

Unit 3: Friends and family

Lesson A: Listening

Exercise 1 page 30

1. grandmother   4. mother
2. daughter   5. father
3. grandfather   6. son

Exercise 2 page 30

1. son   4. grandmother
2. father   5. daughter
3. mother   6. grandfather

Exercise 3 page 31

(L to R:) 1, 2, 5, 6, 4, 3

Exercise 4 page 31

1. mother
2. father
3. daughter
4. son
5. grandmother
6. grandfather

Lesson B: Family members

Exercise 1 page 32

1. sister - brother
2. son - daughter
3. grandmother - grandfather
4. husband - wife
5. mother - father
6. aunt - uncle

Exercise 2 page 32

```
        m
    b r o t h e r
    a u n t
            h u s b a n d
    w i f e
s i s t e r
```

Exercise 3 page 33

1. a
2. a
3. b

Exercise 4 page 33

1. brother
2. sister
3. father
4. mother
5. uncle
6. aunt

Lesson C: Do you have a sister?

Exercise 1 page 34

1. No, we don't.
2. Yes, I do.
3. Yes, we do.
4. No, I don't.
5. Yes, I do.

Exercise 2 page 35

1. sister
2. daughter
3. husband
4. son

Lesson D: Reading

Exercise 1 page 36
1. wife
2. daughter
3. father
4. mother

Exercise 2 page 36
1. No
2. Yes
3. Yes
4. No
5. No

Exercise 3 page 37
Male: boy, man
Female: girl, woman
Male or Female: baby, teenager

Exercise 4 page 37
1. woman
2. man
3. boy
4. girl
5. woman
6. man
7. woman
8. teenager
9. baby

Lesson E: Writing

Exercise 1 page 38
1. wife
2. uncle
3. sister
4. mother
5. daughter
6. grandfather

Exercise 2 page 38
1. uncle
2. sister
3. daughter
4. wife
5. mother
6. grandfather

Exercise 3 page 38
1. father
2. grandfather
3. baby
4. mother
5. grandmother

Exercise 4 page 39
1. father
2. mother
3. brother
4. wife
5. son
6. daughter

Exercise 5 page 39
1. husband
2. son
3. father
4. son
5. brother
6. father

Lesson F: Another view

Exercise 1 page 40
1. B
2. B
3. C
4. A
5. A
6. C

Exercise 2 page 41
1. father
2. aunt
3. son
4. aunt
5. brother
6. wife
7. man

Exercise 3 page 41
w i f e o r d i m b a b y g
o w o m a n r s i s t r v e
s i s t e r s t f l c e l o
c a m e r t m o t h e r n k
h u s b a n d s h o u m k l
n m o w i e t e e n a g e r
u n c l e t b u b f w a p o

Unit 4: Health

Lesson A: Listening

Exercise 1 page 42
1. patient
2. doctor's office
3. nurse
4. medicine
5. doctor
6. patient

Exercise 2 page 43
(L to R:) 1, 5, 2, 3, 4

Exercise 3 page 43
1. doctor's office
2. nurse
3. patient
4. medicine
5. doctor

Lesson B: Parts of the body

Exercise 1 page 44
1. hand
2. head
3. foot
4. arm
5. leg
6. stomach

Exercise 2 page 44
1. stomach
2. arm
3. foot
4. head
5. hand
6. leg

Exercise 3 page 45
1. foot
2. hand
3. head
4. stomach
5. leg
6. arm

Lesson C: My feet hurt.

Exercise 1 page 46
1. eye - eyes
2. hand - hands
3. foot - feet
4. arm - arms
5. leg - legs

Exercise 2 page 46
r e p l e g s t u r
f q b o p h a n d s
o u m j f e e t k e
f o o t t l s c z j
t e r h e a d z y e
a r m s c o m u t r
l e k f t p e y e s

Exercise 3 page 47
1. eye, eyes
2. hand, hands
3. foot, feet
4. leg, legs
5. arm, arms

Exercise 4 page 47

1. legs
2. arm
3. foot
4. hands
5. eyes
6. stomach

Lesson D: Reading

Exercise 1 page 48

1. stomach   4. arm
2. hand   5. leg
3. foot   6. head

Exercise 2 page 49

1. c   3. f   5. a
2. d   4. b   6. e

Exercise 3 page 49

1. toothache
2. headache
3. cold

Lesson E: Writing

Exercise 1 page 50

Across
1. sore throat
4. arm
5. cold
7. eyes

Down
1. stomachache
2. headache
3. toothache
6. legs

Exercise 2 page 51

1. cold
2. fever
3. headache
4. stomachache
5. sore throat

Exercise 3 page 51

1. sore throat
2. cold
3. headache
4. stomachache
5. fever

Lesson F: Another view

Exercise 1 page 52

1. A   4. B
2. B   5. C
3. B   6. A

Exercise 2 page 53

1. hands   4. arms
2. eyes   5. legs
3. feet

Exercise 3 page 53

1. My head
2. My stomach
3. My leg
4. My foot

Unit 5: Around town

Lesson A: Listening

Exercise 1 page 54

1. bank
2. library
3. restaurant
4. supermarket
5. school

Exercise 2 page 55

1. e   4. c
2. a   5. b
3. d

Exercise 3 page 55

1. street   4. library
2. bank   5. restaurant
3. school   6. supermarket

Lesson B: Places around town

Exercise 1 page 56

1. pharmacy
2. movie theater
3. gas station
4. post office
5. laundromat
6. hospital

Exercise 2 page 56

t w j v e a x p b u o y g z
x c j b v g o v x j m p b m
p o s t o f f i c e l u j j
g a s s t a t i o n y h a a
u x c o u j m q h o s p a w
g p u a l a u n d r o m a t
p h a r m a c y l r p m q s
r s o f v a k p o l h d f t
m o v i e t h e a t e r g u
h j p e d y h o s p i t a l
a l a u n d p n g e i o c e

Exercise 3 page 57

1. hospital
2. pharmacy
3. post office
4. movie theater
5. laundromat
6. gas station

Lesson C: The school is on Main Street.

Exercise 1 page 58

1. next to
2. across from
3. next to
4. on
5. between
6. across from
7. across from
8. between

Exercise 2 page 59

1. Next to   3. Between
2. Across from   4. On

Exercise 3 page 59

1. c   3. a   5. b
2. d   4. e

Lesson D: Reading

Exercise 1 page 60

1. bank
2. restaurant
3. pharmacy
4. hospital

Exercise 2 page 60
1. hospital
2. Lake Street
3. bank, pharmacy
4. restaurant

Exercise 3 page 61
1. car   4. bus
2. taxi   5. train
3. bicycle   6. foot

Exercise 4 page 61
Yoko: by taxi
Ted: by bus
Martin: by bicycle
Nadia: by car
Sam: on foot
Katia: by train

Lesson E: Writing

Exercise 1 page 62
1. bank
2. school
3. post office
4. supermarket
5. library

Exercise 2 page 62
1. Third Avenue
2. library
3. bank
4. post office
5. supermarket

Exercise 3 page 63
1. on
2. next to
3. across from
4. on
5. between
6. across from

Lesson F: Another view

Exercise 1 page 64
1. A   4. B
2. B   5. A
3. C   6. A

Exercise 2 page 65
1. b a n k (b u s) s t r e e t c a r
2. t r a i n f o o t (t a x i) b a n k
3. t a x i b u s (t r a i n) c e n t e r
4. l i b r a r y (b i c y c l e) f o o t
5. c a r a c r o s s (f o o t) t a x i
6. s h o p s t o r e (c a r) p o s t

Exercise 3 page 65
1. Excuse me
2. Thanks
3. Where's the supermarket
4. Next to the pharmacy

Unit 6: Time

Lesson A: Listening

Exercise 1 page 66
1. 10:00   4. 6:30
2. 2:30   5. 9:00
3. 7:00   6. 10:30

Exercise 2 page 66
1. 2:30
2. 9:00
3. 10:30
4. 7:00

Exercise 3 page 67

Lesson B: Events

Exercise 1 page 68
1. 4:30, Monday
2. 3:30, Tuesday
3. 9:30, Wednesday
4. 5:00, Thursday

Exercise 2 page 68
1. class   4. meeting
2. movie   5. appointment
3. party   6. show

Exercise 3 page 69
1A. meeting
1B. 10:00
2A. party
2B. 8:30
3A. class
3B. 11:00
4A. appointment
4B. 3:30
5A. movie
5B. 7:30
6A. TV show
6B. 9:00

Lesson C: Is your class at 11:00?

Exercise 1 page 70
1. No, it isn't. It's at 11:00 a.m.
2. No, it isn't. It's at 7:45 p.m.
3. Yes, it is.
4. No, it isn't. It's at 8:00 p.m.
5. Yes, it is.

Exercise 2 page 71
1. No, it isn't.
2. No, it isn't.
3. Yes, it is.
4. No, it isn't.
5. Yes, it is.

Exercise 3 page 71
1. appointment - five o'clock
2. meeting - three o'clock
3. movie - seven o'clock
4. party - nine o'clock
5. class - eight-thirty

Lesson D: Reading

Exercise 1 page 72
6: his sister's birthday party.
2: his doctor's appointment.
1: his favorite TV show.
5: his concert.
4: his English class.
3: his meeting with Abram.

Exercise 2 page 72
1. At 10:30   4. At 7:30
2. At 12:00   5. At 5:00
3. At 1:00   6. At 8:00

Exercise 3 page 73
1. d   2. c   3. a   4. b

Exercise 4 page 73
1. d   3. b   5. a
2. e   4. f   6. c

Exercise 5 page 73
1. in the morning
2. in the afternoon
3. at night
4. at noon
5. in the evening
6. at midnight

Lesson E: Writing

Exercise 1 page 74
1. party
2. appointment
3. TV show
4. class
5. movie
6. meeting

Exercise 2 page 75
1. appointment
2. class
3. 3:30
4. 8:30

Exercise 3 page 75
10:30 – appointment
1:00 – class
3:30 – meeting
8:30 – party

Lesson F: Another view

Exercise 1 page 76
1. A   2. B   3. C   4. C

Exercise 2 page 77
1. party
2. class
3. evening
4. morning
5. midnight

Exercise 3 page 77
```
m e l a p p o n o b o m
i n t e v e n i n g f o
p a r t y l i s h z a v
i n g w e n c l a s s p
g m o r n i n g i n o r
c o n c m i d n i g h t
```

Unit 7: Shopping

Lesson A: Listening

Exercise 1 page 78
1. a shirt   4. a T-shirt
2. socks   5. a dress
3. shoes   6. pants

Exercise 2 page 78
1. a shirt
2. a T-shirt
3. a dress
4. pants
5. socks
6. shoes

Exercise 3 page 79
1. shoes   4. T-shirt
2. dress   5. shirt
3. socks   6. pants

Exercise 4 page 79
Down   **Across**
1. shoes   5. shirt
2. T-shirt   6. socks
3. pants
4. dress

Lesson B: Clothing

Exercise 1 page 80
1. a tie   4. a jacket
2. a sweater   5. a raincoat
3. a skirt   6. a blouse

Exercise 2 page 80
1. raincoat   4. blouse
2. skirt   5. tie
3. jacket   6. sweater

Exercise 3 page 81
1. $25.99   4. blouse
2. raincoat   5. $24.50
3. $42.50   6. jacket

Lesson C: How much are the shoes?

Exercise 1 page 82
1. a   4. a
2. b   5. c
3. c   6. b

Exercise 2 page 82
1. is   4. are
2. are   5. are
3. is   6. is

Exercise 3 page 83
1A. is   4A. is
1B. $42.00   4B. $36.50
2A. are   5A. is
2B. $45.00   5B. $35.00
3A. are   6A. is
3B. $3.50   6B. $27.50

Lesson D: Reading

Exercise 1 page 84

1. No
2. Yes
3. Yes
4. Yes
5. No

Exercise 2 page 84

white: shirt
blue: pants, tie
black: shoes, socks

Exercise 3 page 85

1. Black
2. Yellow
3. Red
4. White
5. Black
6. Brown
7. Blue
8. Green

Lesson E: Writing

Exercise 1 page 86

1. blouse
2. raincoat
3. jacket
4. tie
5. sweater
6. skirt

Exercise 2 page 86

1. blouse
2. tie
3. raincoat
4. skirt
5. jacket
6. sweater

Exercise 3 page 87

Men's clothes: tie
Men's and women's clothes:
jacket, pants, raincoat,
shoes, socks, sweater
Women's clothes: blouse,
dress, skirt

Exercise 4 page 87

Francesca: shoes
Lisa: raincoat
Jerome: pants
Carmela: dress
Mario: shirt

Lesson F: Another view

Exercise 1 page 88

Clothing

tie
shirt
pants
shoes
Total: $123.00

Exercise 2 page 89

```
s w e s h o j a c r
p r i n g r e e n d
t e c y e l l o w g
k a t h r e d l n o
b l a c k m b l u e
c o l s c h o b l u
s h a w h i t e r o
a i n c t s h i b l
n m p b r o w n e c
r o r a n g e s o c
p i n k d r e p a s
o u s e p u r p l e
```

Exercise 3 page 89

1. pants
2. shoes
3. T-shirt
4. pants
5. tie

Unit 8: Work

Lesson A: Listening

Exercise 1 page 90

1. mechanic
2. server
3. salesperson
4. receptionist
5. custodian
6. cashier

Exercise 2 page 90

```
t r c a m n i v z q u i
s a l e s p e r s o n t
e c t r o k j u m g l u
p t o s e r v e r t u h
c a s h i e r e n o s l
l i e s t w a p s h e a
r e c e p t i o n i s t
r o n p e c i k m a r r
c c u s t o d i a n t e
i e u z t i o n w a i z
k m e c h a n i c g o s
```

Exercise 3 page 91

Top row: 2, 4, 6
Bottom row: 1, 3, 5

1. salesperson
2. receptionist
3. custodian
4. cashier
5. mechanic
6. server

Exercise 4 page 91

1. Fatima - receptionist
2. Cecilia - salesperson
3. Bruno - custodian
4. Gabriel - waiter
5. Cathy - mechanic
6. Edward - cashier

Lesson B: Job duties

Exercise 1 page 92

server: serves food
mechanic: fixes cars
salesperson: sells clothes
receptionist: answers the phone
custodian: cleans buildings
cashier: counts money

Exercise 2 page 92

1. serves food
2. answers the phone
3. counts money
4. sells clothes
5. cleans buildings
6. fixes cars

Exercise 3 page 92

1. fixes cars
2. sells clothes
3. serves food

Exercise 4 page 93

1. sells clothes
2. cleans buildings
3. counts money
4. serves food
5. answers the phone
6. fixes cars

Lesson C: Does he sell clothes?

Exercise 1 page 94

1. a
2. a
3. b
4. a
5. b
6. a

Exercise 2 page 95

1A. Does, serve
1B. does
2A. Does, count
2B. does
3A. Does, answer
3B. doesn't
4A. Does, clean
4B. does
5A. Does, fix
5B. doesn't
6A. Does, sell
6B. does

Lesson D: Reading

Exercise 1 page 96

1. sells clothes, salesperson
2. fixes cars, mechanic
3. helps the teacher, teacher's aide
4. serves food, waiter
5. answers the phone, receptionist

Exercise 2 page 97

1. truck driver
2. homemaker
3. plumber
4. teacher's aide
5. bus driver
6. painter

Lesson E: Writing

Exercise 1 page 98

1. sells
2. counts
3. serves
4. fixes
5. cleans
6. drives

Exercise 2 page 98

1. clothes
2. food
3. buildings
4. money
5. cars
6. bus
7. phone

Exercise 3 page 98

1. custodian, buildings
2. cashier, money
3. bus driver, bus

Exercise 4 page 99

1. server
2. serves
3. bus driver
4. drives
5. salesperson
6. sell

Exercise 5 page 99

1. Rita
2. Tamar
3. Levon

Lesson F: Another view

Exercise 1 page 100

1. A
2. C
3. B
4. A
5. B
6. A

Exercise 2 page 101

```
m e c h a n i c
        o
        m
    s e r v e r
p l u m b e r
      p a i n t e r
          k
c a s h i e r
  b u s d r i v e r
```

Exercise 3 page 101

1. bus driver, drives a bus
2. cashier, counts money
3. mechanic, fixes cars
4. truck driver, drives a truck

Unit 9: Daily living

Lesson A: Listening

Exercise 1 page 102

1. dishes
2. homework
3. lunch
4. laundry
5. bed
6. dishes

Exercise 2 page 102

1. making lunch
2. doing homework
3. washing the dishes

Exercise 3 page 102

1. washing
2. making
3. doing
4. drying
5. making
6. doing

Exercise 4 page 103

(L to R:) 2, 6, 3, 5, 1, 4

Exercise 5 page 103

1. drying the dishes
2. doing the laundry
3. doing homework
4. washing the dishes
5. making lunch
6. making the bed

Lesson B: Outside chores

Exercise 1 page 104
1. cutting
2. getting
3. taking out
4. walking
5. watering
6. washing

Exercise 2 page 104
1. cutting the grass
2. taking out the trash
3. getting the mail
4. walking the dog
5. watering the grass
6. washing the car

Exercise 3 page 105
1. Watering
2. Cutting
3. Getting
4. Washing
5. Taking out
6. Walking

Lesson C: What are they doing?

Exercise 1 page 106
1. drying the dishes
2. making the bed
3. getting the mail
4. taking out the trash
5. washing the car
6. doing the laundry
7. cutting the grass
8. walking the dog

Exercise 2 page 106
1A. are
1B. mail
2A. is
2B. dinner
3A. is
3B. grass
4A. are
4B. dishes
5A. is
5B. dog
6A. is
6B. trash

Exercise 3 page 107
1A. is
1B. Making
2A. are
2B. Making
3A. is
3B. Getting
4A. are
4B. Cutting
5A. is
5B. Washing
6A. is
6B. Taking

Lesson D: Reading

Exercise 1 page 108
1. No
2. Yes
3. No
4. Yes
5. Yes

Exercise 2 page 108
1. washing the car
2. washing the dishes
3. cutting the grass
4. doing homework
5. taking out the trash

Exercise 3 page 109
1. bathroom
2. bedroom
3. living room
4. laundry room
5. kitchen
6. dining room

Exercise 4 page 109
1. kitchen
2. bedroom
3. kitchen
4. laundry room
5. kitchen

Lesson E: Writing

Exercise 1 page 110
1. drying
2. washing
3. making
4. doing
5. making
6. doing

Exercise 2 page 110
1. doing homework
2. making the bed
3. drying the dishes
4. washing the dishes
5. doing the laundry
6. making lunch

Exercise 3 page 111
Justin: doing the laundry
Melissa: washing the dishes
Henry: doing homework
Penny: making lunch
Bill: making the bed
Erica: drying the dishes

Lesson F: Another view

Exercise 1 page 112
1. B
2. A
3. C
4. A
5. C

Exercise 2 page 112
1. is washing
2. is making
3. is taking out
4. is cutting
5. is doing

Exercise 3 page 113
1. bathroom
2. bedroom
3. kitchen
4. dining room
5. living room
6. laundry room

Exercise 4 page 113
1. kitchen
2. laundry room
3. kitchen
4. bedroom
5. kitchen

Exercise 5 page 113
Chores inside the house: drying the dishes, making lunch, making the bed, washing the dishes

Chores outside the house: cutting the grass, walking the dog, washing the car, watering the grass

Unit 10: Free time

Lesson A: Listening

Exercise 1 page 114
1. fish
2. swim
3. dance
4. exercise
5. play cards
6. play basketball

Exercise 2 page 114
b i c y t a b l s h
p (d a n c e) y z f i
e x e r (p l a y) m b
(e x e r c i s e) d o
(c a r d s) m o n w t
e y f i (s w i m) y a
d a v n g e l u s w
n c (f i s h) i m b a
(b a s k e t b a l l)
d s z o n f r e x p

Exercise 3 page 115
(L to R:) 2, 4, 5, 1, 3
1. swim
2. play basketball
3. play cards
4. fish
5. exercise

Lesson B: Around the house

Exercise 1 page 116
1. read magazines
2. play the guitar
3. listen to music
4. watch TV
5. work in the garden

Exercise 2 page 116
1. music
2. TV
3. the guitar
4. in the garden
5. magazines

Exercise 3 page 117
1. Cook
2. Listen to music
3. Read magazines
4. Play the guitar
5. Work in the garden
6. Watch TV

Lesson C: I like to watch TV.

Exercise 1 page 118
1. likes   5. like
2. likes   6. like
3. like   7. likes
4. likes   8. like

Exercise 2 page 119
1. likes, exercise
2. likes, cook
3. likes, swim
4. likes, fish
5. like, dance
6. like, play cards

Lesson D: Reading

Exercise 1 page 120
1. Yes   4. No
2. No   5. Yes
3. No   6. Yes

Exercise 2 page 121
1. volunteer
2. go to the movies
3. exercise
4. travel
5. shop

Lesson E: Writing

Exercise 1 page 122
1. swim   4. shop
2. fish   5. dance
3. cook   6. volunteer

Exercise 2 page 122
1. work in the garden
2. swim
3. volunteer

4. fish
5. play cards

Exercise 3 page 123
1. play   5. visit
2. watch   6. exercise
3. read   7. listen to
4. go

Exercise 4 page 123
Sunday: go to the movies
Monday: exercise
Tuesday: listen to music
Wednesday: read magazines
Thursday: watch TV
Friday: visit friends
Saturday: play basketball

Lesson F: Another view

Exercise 1 page 124
1. A   4. A
2. C   5. B
3. B   6. A

Exercise 2 page 125
1. play cards
2. visit friends
3. play the guitar
4. read magazines
5. play basketball
6. listen to music

Exercise 3 page 125
Costs money: travel, go to the movies, shop
No money: run, visit friends, volunteer

Exercise 4 page 125
Exercise: dance, play basketball, play soccer, run, swim
No exercise: go online, listen to music, play cards, read magazines, watch TV

Illustration credits

John Batten: 21, 29, 36, 48, 49 (b), 98, 107, 115
Kevin Brown: 3, 22, 50, 59, 63, 72, 73, 111
Kim Johnson: 33, 38, 45, 97
Frank Montagna: 26, 44, 53, 69, 80, 91, 95, 117
Scott Mooney: 35, 46, 61, 104, 121
Paul Hampson: 34, 47 (t), 78 (t), 85, 116

Ben Hasler: 39, 57, 81, 86, 109
Q2A Media Services: 5 (#6), 8, 19, 20, 23, 31, 43, 47 (b), 55, 62, 66 (t), 67, 72 (br), 78 (b), 88, 103
Bill Waitzman: 27, 49 (t), 83, 92, 112
Phil Williams: 5, 58

Photography credits

Cover front (tl) Andrew Zarivny/Shutterstock, (tr) Stuart Monk/Shutterstock, (r) Gary D Ercole/Photolibrary/Getty Images, (cr) Sam Kolich; (br) Nathan Maxfield/iStockphoto, (c) Monkey Business Images/Shutterstock, (bl) Alistair Forrester Shankie/iStockphoto, (cl) ML Harris/Iconica/Getty Images, (l) Mark Lewis/Digital Vision/Getty Images, back (tc) cloki/Shutterstock (br) gualtiero boffi/Shutterstock

6 (tl) ©Jason Stitt/Shutterstock

10 (tl) ©konstantynov/Shutterstock, (tr) ©Sanja Deva/Shutterstock

11 (t) ©Comstock/thinkstock

14 (t) ©szefei/Shutterstock

15 (b) ©DEKANARYAS/Shutterstock

18 (br) ©Kitch Bain/Shutterstock, (tl) ©Serg64/Shutterstock, (cl) ©juat/Shutterstock, (bl) ©oznuroz/Shutterstock

30 (tl) ©luna4/Shutterstock, (tr) ©Golden Pixels LLC/Shutterstock, (cl) © Diego Cervo/Shutterstock, (cr) ©S.Borisov/Shutterstock, (bl) ©Andres Rodriguez/Fotolia, (br) ©Marta Nardini/Getty Images

32 (b) ©Andresr/Shutterstock

41 (bl) ©Monkey Business Images/Shutterstock

42 (tl) ©Andersen Ross/Getty Images, (tr) ©Andersen Ross/Getty Images, (cl) ©wavebreakmedia/Shutterstock, (cr) ©Rob Byron/Shutterstock, 42 (bl) ©michaeljung/Shutterstock, (br) ©Halfdark/Getty Images

54 (tl) ©Cynthia Farmer/Shutterstock, (br) ©Erik Isakson/Tetra Images/Corbis, (tcl) ©TommL/iStockphoto, (bcl) ©CandyBox Images/Shutterstock, (bl) ©Monkey Business Images/Shutterstock

65 (bcl) ©Henry Westheim Photography/Alamy

79 (tl) ©zhaoyan/Shutterstock, (tcl) ©Gemenacom/Shutterstock, (bcl) ©largeformat4x5 /iStockphoto, (bl) ©kedrov/Shutterstock, (tc) ©Coloss/Shutterstock, (cr) ©Olga Popova/Shutterstock

93 (tl) ©Glow Images, Inc/Getty Image, (tr) ©Tim Hall/Getty Image, (cl) ©Masterfile, (cr) ©auremar/Shtterstock, (bl) ©Norman Pogson/Shutterstock, (br) ©fatihhoca/iStockphoto

94 (cr) ©Ron Fehling/Masterfile, (tl) ©Levent Konuk/Shutterstock, (tr) ©Blend Images/Shutterstock, (cl) ©Gene Chutka/iStockphoto, (bl) ©Blend_Images/iStockphoto, (br) ©wavebreakmedia/Shutterstock

99 (cl) ©Brand X Pictures/Thinkstock, (tl) ©Push/Getty Images, (bl) ©Dmitry Kalinovsky/iStockphoto

102 (cl) ©Jupiterimages/Getty Images, (c) ©greenland/Shutterstock, (cr) ©Elenathewise/Fotolia

105 (tl) ©Ned Frisk/Blend Images/Alamy, (tr) ©katja kodba/Shuttestock, (cl) ©amana productions inc./Getty Images, (cr) ©Hemera/Thinkstock, (bl) ©RCWW, Inc./RCWW, Inc./Corbis, (br) ©Echo/Getty Images

108 (br) ©Corbis Premium RF/Alamy

118 (tc) ©Kinga/Shutterstock

119 (tl) ©tankist276/Shutterstock, (tr) ©Jupiterimages/Thinkstock, (cl) ©Ana Abejon/iStockphoto, (cr) ©Pavol Kmeto/Shutterstock, (bl) ©Erik Isakson/Corbis, (br) ©AVAVA/Shutterstock

120 (tl) ©Westend61 - WEST/Getty Images, (tc) ©Comstock/Getty Images, (tr) ©Karin Dreyer/Getty Images